ENDORSEMENTS

The Republic of South Africa has eleven official languages. In SeTswana, one of the official languages, there is a proverb that says "Kgosi ke Kgosi ka batho", meaning "A King is only a King for the People and to serve the people". Leadership is about serving others skillfully and with a wholehearted commitment. The proverb makes a strong case for the need for righteous servant leaders who will serve people instead of desiring to be served. Apostle Eric L. Warren makes the same persuasive case in his book: *Ten Times Better*. He not only makes the case, but also gives us a solid Kingdom blueprint with biblical guidance on how to raise up such leaders.

The nations of the world need transformational leaders who will bring sustainable change and development to their communities and nations. It needs leaders who will teach, train and equip others to do the same. Apostle Warren is himself such a leader. He has lived and demonstrated the biblical model of servant and transformational leadership over the decades. He is a tried, tested and true leader who has mentored and continues to mentor many leaders and upcoming leaders around the world.

This book is a must have for every Bible school, school of ministry and for all leaders and leaders in training. I do not hesitate to recommend and endorse this book which will renew and transform your mindset and change the leadership narrative globally.

Dr. Pearl Kupe, International President,
Global Forum of Women Entrepreneurs Johannesburg, South Africa

There is no doubt that the Babylonian system has become more attractive and seductive over the years. More and more we are witnessing how Babylon sells opportunity in exchange for the soul.

Apostle Eric Warren introduces us to tried and tested principles that not only helps the believer to survive Babylon but ignites the believer to thrive in Babylon and ultimately conquer Babylon.

The concept of "*Ten Times Better*" is deeply rooted in values and principles that are amplified in the life of a kingdom change agent who understands self-governance and kingdom agendas.

Our dilemma in confronting 21st century Babylonian systems is that we send in soldiers who have not mastered the above. They are engaging the systems of this world with an appetite for worldliness that has not been quelled by the spirit of God. In this book we see how a revelation on King-Priest dimension sets us up for success and conquest in Babylon. Daniel and co are used as a prototype of kingdom ingenuity. In them we see a working pattern and more importantly we learn that Babylon can be conquered.

"*Ten Times better*" is a mindset and a spirit that must be operative in every generation of church. As you imbibe the wisdom of this book, my prayer is that you will become TEN TIMES BETTER where God has placed you. What we urgently need is a manifestation of God's kingdom in the corridors of power and such can only come through a King-Priest prototype that is ten times better.

Apostle Brandon Bailey, Senior Elder- Teleios Church, Johannesburg, South Africa Lead Apostle- KIN Network

Apostle Eric Warren's book "*Ten Times Better*", is an important, timely resource for the people of God. At a time when many are focused upon and talking about the Kingdom of God, Apostle Warren provides revelatory teaching and practical instruction regarding the importance and character of sons and daughters as princes, kings and priests in God's Kingdom.

Utilizing the story of Daniel, Apostle Warren mines deep revelatory insight, that calls a generation from compromise to clarity, commitment to God and excellence. *"Ten Times Better"* is an engaging book, that is easy to read, with good flow and real depth. Written with a great combination of scriptural instruction, biblical principles and personal life experiences, Apostle Warren provides seasoned wisdom in a resource that can be applied personally, or that can be re-taught as a valuable church resource for leaders.

This is a book with strategic importance and important timing to re-focus God's people on foundational principles that can have genuine generational impact. It is one that I recommend and will be referencing again for myself and our church congregation.

DR. GREGORY REYNOLDS, Senior Pastor, House of Liberty
Covenant Church, Cincinnati, Ohio

Over the last two decades, I have been a student of Apostle Warren through his social media platforms, seminars and books which have had great impact on my life. It is with great honor to endorse his latest book, *Ten Times Better: Strategies for Developing Daniel-Type Change Agents.*

Living in the Realm of Ten Times Better is a message that is relevant for our times. It provides a template to encourage and assess where we are, rediscover our purpose, propel us into new dimensions, and provokes us to be intentional in developing spiritual sons and daughters. His practical application, personal stories/testimonies, and insights from the Holy Spirit are profound and resourceful, allowing us to embrace Kingdom values and challenging us to model excellence in character.

As one that has been in the market place over 45 years in various capacities of leadership these transferable truths will help to keep us on the cutting edge, producing results in every arena of our lives.

Why settle for the norm when we can live a life that's *Ten Times Better?*

ANITA F. DAWSON, Apostle, Columbus, Ohio

TEN TIMES BETTER

Preparing a New Generation of Daniel-Type Leaders

By Eric L. Warren

DEDICATION

R ECENTLY I MADE A STATEMENT TO THE CONGREGATION that I formerly pastored. I said: "I have already surpassed everything that I ever imagined that I would do when I was a young man." You might say that maybe my vision was too small, and you would probably be correct. But it is a fact that my upbringing did not instill in me a large vision for my potential. So, today I marvel at the life that the Lord has graced me to live. My primary gratefulness centers around my family. My wife has been an inestimable gift to me and my children, to whom I dedicate this book, have been my heart's delight.

God blessed us with three delightful, charming, intelligent girls that are the pride of my life. They are biological daughters and spiritual sons. They carry our DNA in spirit, soul, and body. For me, they each minister to me personally in three unique and special ways. I value them as people, not simply as my daughters.

The principles that I have endeavored to expound upon in this book are principles that my wife and I have endeavored to deposit into their lives. They have embraced these principles, and they are endeavoring to live lives that represent the "ten times better" grace that was on the Prophet Daniel.

And so, I dedicate this book to my daughters: Ebony (Warren) Tye, Charisse (Warren) Austin, and Monica Warren. May you live long and be strong in the ways of the Lord. And may you grow exponentially in the ten times better way of life. Thank you for fulfilling my life-long dream of being a father...

Love you,

Dad

FOREWORD

THE CHURCH IS AN ASSEMBLAGE OF INDIVIDUALS WHO have submitted their lives to Jesus Christ. When the Church is assembled in accordance to the eternal purpose and architecture set out in the Holy Scriptures, it functions as God's Holy Nation. A very special generation of people, chosen to be God's treasure trove on earth. Each member is granted the right of access to the realm of divine privilege, assured of enjoying unfair advantages in this present world order. But such advantages are premised by compliance to righteous standards clearly set out in the Word of God.

The Holy Scriptures graphically describes the Church, being clothed with every blessing and grace, the divine investiture for her to be the gene pool of resource to the nations. Therefore the Church should efficaciously produce sons and daughters who are light and salt to the earth.

Regrettably, the present global Covid-19 pandemic has highlighted the scarcity of godly leadership, especially those who intimately know the Father, His ways and doings. The absence of such leaders has muted the counsel of God and thereby contributed to the subsequent chaos in the Church and the World. In perilous times, ideally the way should be paved for the emergence of a 'Daniel order' who definitively speaks to the hierarchy of the Church and World. As Psalm 23 states, 'thy rod and staff they comfort me' in the 'valley of the shadow of death'. Sadly, this is not so! We do not see governmental/apostolic (rod) and statesmanlike/elder (staff) leaders emerging to guide us through these turbulent times.

For us to raise leaders of the caliber of Daniel, we should ascertain the root causality for the shortage of leaders. Why has the Church dismally failed to inculcate godly leaders? Why is it that those from within our ranks who become successful, succumb to being subdued and castigated by Babylonian systems of rule? This review should comparatively establish the difference in approach, between the present-day Church and that in biblical times.

Another plausible area of comparison is the epistemological foundations of the Twenty-First Century Church to the prescribed biblical blueprint. We should seriously evaluate the prevailing phenomenon utilized to raise godly leaders. Many Church traditions have adopted contemporary modes, namely, entertainment, performance, commercial and personality. Others have utilized traditional, institutional and historical Church modes. Finally, there is the Apostolic movement currently searching the Scriptures to extract eternal principles which can be incarnated into workable templates that would produce the sons of God. Like Daniel, such people would not recant on their faith and conviction of their election and calling. Their assignment is to represent their Heavenly Father through their vocations in this world.

Inquiry for fresh biblical prototypes will demand new searches through the Scriptures to discover the mind and counsel of God. For example, in historical biblical settings the family was the place where children were raised by godly fathers and mothers to fulfil the divine mandate. These households headed by fathers instilled the Law of God into their children. They understood the covenant and its conditions entered into between God and their patriarchal fathers. They knew they were established as a covenant people to represent God in the earth. They simply believed they were a unique breed of people in the earth.

Eric L. Warren has accurately discerned the gaping need of our times...an alarming absence of godly leaders in the Church and Society. At the heart of his thesis is the conviction that unless the Church raises godly leaders, the earth and its inhabitants will remain in darkness. He shifts the horizon of the reader by proposing a biblical example of the caliber of leaders the Church should be raising. The case study of Daniel is brilliantly analyzed, key principles extrapolated and then craftily narrated. The undergirding objective is to simply unveil the potential locked up in each member of the Church. A potential which can be attained in Christ.

Ten Times Better is a clarion call for the Households in the Church to comprehend the quality of leaders that should be produced. Contained in its chapters are detailed features of the life and ministry of Daniel. We find a carefully constructed list of characteristics distinguishing the spirit, nature and behavior of those who are in Christ. Presented are the limits and standards that every child of God should aspire after. They challenge those in Church leadership to make this their goal in ministry, to raise the Sons of God to occupy the gates of cities or fields of expertise for the transformation of the world.

At the heart of Eric's message is the drive to shift the paradigm of the institutional way of 'doing church!' There must be a concerted move to migrate from the religious mentality of merely gathering to worship to that of gathering as a family for the purpose of generating a breed of people and leaders whose vocational service in the world stands head and shoulders above their contemporaries. Such leaders live from the realm of the eternal, governed by the Spirit and mantled with every grace to outrun horses.

Eric has been my friend for many years. I've learnt to respect his immaculate and principled approach to life as a whole, his strong endearing marriage, his prolific writing skills and the stately elegance in which he conducts himself. Yet for as long as I've known him, a dominant aspect of his life has been an advocacy for raising leaders to represent Christ in every facet of society. Every part of his being oozes with the passion to train leaders. For him this is a critical element in changing the world we live in. He has cried out to the church to reconsider its ways. To bring the Church back to the apostolic patterns set out in Scripture.

I believe that *Ten Times Better* is a present truth word from the throne. Those who read it will be provoked to rethink the purpose for the establishment of the Church and her role in the earth. I anticipate that it could incite serious conversations on the Church's *modus operandi* and hierarchical structure so that fresh biblical systems and environmental conditions are created for the Daniel type of leader to emerge.

Thamo Naidoo

GATE GLOBAL FAMILY
SANDTON, SOUTH AFRICA

CONTENTS

CHAPTER ONE

RAISING KINGS
THAT CHANGE CULTURE

P ERHAPS AT NO OTHER TIME IN MODERN HISTORY DO WE
see the need for the Body of Christ to return to the mindset of intentionally developing sons and daughters who represent King Jesus. We are living in times when the entire world,
not just a nation, can suffer from the evil decisions of a bad
leader. The world has become a global community, and that is
no clearer than the recent events of the greatest pandemic of our
lifetimes. Conversely society as a whole can also benefit from
the righteous decisions of a Godly leader. But where do we find
such leaders? I submit to you that the best leaders are developed in the Kingdom of God with Kingdom values, Kingdom
character, and Kingdom excellence. In the Kingdom of God,
we find the best values, the best intellect, the best wisdom, the

best motives, the best character, etc. Those reared under the environmental influences of the Kingdom of God, carry the most significant potential for ruling as kings and priests on earth.

Leading and ruling are not for the faint of heart. There is no greater responsibility in life than leading and governing others. Most people see these assignments from the vantage point of the honor and the status that they bring. But the honor and status of any leadership role pale by comparison to the responsibility of that role.

In Biblical times, and even before those times, leaders were prepared from birth; whether for kingship, priesthood, or the marketplace, before allowed to govern anyone. This template has changed over the years, and much of the holistic training and development for leadership has been replaced by academic degrees. I believe we can demonstrate in every discipline that academic degrees and certifications have not necessarily been able to produce good leaders. While academic training has provided the hard, intellectual skills of proficiency in particular disciplines, it has failed in supplying the all-important "soft" skills that are so critical for success as a leader. By soft skills, I mean things like wisdom, compassion, empathy, intuition, common sense, decorum, a sense of fairness and equity, justice, judgment, and the spirit of excellence. Some of these skill sets are categorized as intangibles because they are not easily measured. But their presence or absence can mean the difference between success or failure for a leader.

Many of these intangible skill sets are seen in the training of high-level leadership environments that prepare their people for ruling in the gates of nations, industries, governments, and economies. Beyond the academic vita lies the immeasurable qualities of "Kings" who are bred into a person, more than born into a person. Creating the environment that successfully produces kings and queens requires a special talent and insight that incorporates the best of the wisdom of the ages with the best of the changing culture of the present and future. The Biblical environments of the kingship and the priesthood specialized in producing high caliber leaders in this regard, even though they could not govern the heart of those who were so trained.

God's Template for Modern Kings and Priests

In this book, I want to explore the qualities of excellence, integrity, and righteousness that dwelled in a man called Daniel, the *Old Testament* Prophet. My purpose for doing so is to rediscover ancient pathways to producing people who are able to live in a superlative realm, naturally and spiritually.

In the introduction to the story of Daniel's life in Babylon, we find several principles for developing people with "kingly qualities" who will help us in our quest to establish a people in our current epoch that will also be called "ten times better." Today is the perfect time to shift the focus of the Church from producing believers with a salvation centric mentality to a King-Priest centric mentality. The following is an expanded translation of 1 Peter 2:9, from the *N.T. Expanded Translation* by Greek Scholar, Kenneth Wuest:

> "But as for you, you are a race chosen out, king-priests, a set-apart nation, a people formed for [God's own] possession, in order that you might proclaim abroad the excellencies of the One who out of darkness called you into participation in His marvelous light, who at one time were not a people but now are God's people."

Daniel is an *Old Testament* type of the *New Testament* King-Priest order. He was a man uniquely gifted by virtue of his natural and spiritual training before he ever arrived in the court of Nebuchadnezzar. His personal character, intellect, and spiritual acumen were responsible for catapulting him from the position of slave held captive in the King's court to second in command under three national leaders. My quest in this book is to determine what principles were present in the life of Daniel that enabled him to advance to such prominence and to determine how we may extract glean from these principles to replicate the same caliber of believers today.

I intend to uncover a template, if you will, for understanding how to live what I am calling a ***ten times better life.*** We see this way of life modeled in the *Old Testament,* specifically through the prophet Daniel, and his friends, who are commonly known by their adopted names, Shadrach, Meshack, and Abednego.

In some respect, we can highlight ways in which we live better than our spiritual forefathers, but regarding spiritual matters, it is evident that we are still trying to catch up to the dynamic of their walk with the Father. Regarding the king-priest dimension of the earthly expression of the kingdom, men like Daniel, Joseph, King David, and King Solomon were light years ahead of us. Each of these men had a practical relationship with God, who enabled them to be leaders and rulers who demonstrated a measure of earthly excellence rule that we still try to emulate today. Our mandate to reign and rule with authority and dominion of our God is neither a fable nor is it merely *Old Testament* lore. It is a present reality that we must practically rediscover. If it was possible to walk in harmony with a righteous God and simultaneously rule in high places in earthly systems in the *Old Testament*, then it is undoubtedly attainable and preferred in our current administration.

Daniel was a Kingdom Change Agent

There are a lot of transformative things happening in our society that indicate a tremendous need for the men, women, and children of God to wake up, rise up, and be the transformational change agents befitting of the sons of God. Each day brings a new set of challenges to the principles of the Kingdom of God and the spirit of righteousness. As we take a look at the first chapter of the Book of Daniel, we will discover principles that were resident in the life of Daniel and his friends who enabled them to represent the Kingdom of God as they rose from slavery to dominion. I believe that this journey will challenge us, as the people of God, to live in a higher realm of practical and spiritual effectiveness. We are going to learn to live in a new realm called "ten times better." By exploring the text in the first chapter of the Book of Daniel, we will discover the keys and principles that enabled him to be ten times better in a hostile atmosphere. These principles can also be employed by the sons and daughters of God today.

Quite often, we find that the Church of Jesus Christ is left reacting to the things that are happening around us, rather than being proactive. This must change because we were never designed to be a reactionary force but designed to be a transformative force here on earth. But to make the transition from being reactive to being proactive, we will have to commit to preparing ourselves and our seed for ruling and reigning in every aspect of life. Religion has taught us that we can be at peace with God by engaging in religious activities. But God has not called us to be simply at peace with Him; instead, we are also called to represent Him in our earthly lives. God is powerful, triumphant, righteous, excellent in all His ways, loving, wise, and preeminent in every way. We have the privilege to represent Him on earth while walking in the same principles in our character and harnessing the power of God.

According to the Word of the Lord in Ephesians Chapter 6, "We wrestle not against flesh and blood but against principalities, powers, and rulers of the darkness of this world." In this present age, there is a clear presence of the rulers of darkness in our world. The Bible says that we are wrestling against these dark forces. That means that we are not wrestling against people. We are not wrestling against politicians. We are not wrestling against races, cultures, or even different ideologies, ultimately. We are wrestling with demonic principalities and powers from the dark realm of the spirit. Daniel was in a similar battle in his day with a Babylonian King who wanted to prepare him for servitude in the King's palace. We are going to take a look at how a Godly man wrestles with spiritual forces in a very graphic way and emerges triumphant over them.

Tyrannical Leadership Uses People

One of the things which typify the carnal nature of natural-minded men is the tendency to want to dominate, subjugate, and oppress other men (mankind). This tendency has been pervasive in the history of man and has produced some of the most tyrannical leaders known throughout history. The worst historical of the Pharaohs, the Caesars, and the dictators have this one thing in common - they were narcissistic controllers with an insatiable appetite for receiving worship from their constituents and exercising dominion over them. Their mode of operation was not to give but to take. Their focus was never on what was best for others, but always on what was best for themselves. This is not a leadership construct that honors God. It is a leadership construct that honors the leader and misuses the people under their authority.

We find this same personality type represented by the Babylonian King Nebuchadnezzar. By all accounts, this King was more focused on his internal needs than the needs of those whom he served. As we discover in the first chapter of Daniel, Nebuchadnezzar's desire for domination led to Daniel's capture and the enslavement of the people of God. In this chapter, we will discover the intentions of that enslavement by Nebuchadnezzar, and we will also learn the dominant power of God at work in the lives of men who committed their entire lives to be faithful to Jehovah God.

The King of Babylon Wants to Steal the Sons of God

Daniel 1:1, "In the third year of the reign of Jehoiakim King of Judah came Nebuchadnezzar King of Babylon unto Jerusalem and besieged it."

Beloved saints, I want you to know that the Kings of Babylon (the world order separated from Jehovah God) are endeavoring to siege Jerusalem (the Church of Jesus Christ) today. The greatest treasure of any government is its people. Therefore, Nebuchadnezzar seized Jerusalem primarily so that he could capture its people and bring them into his service. The government in and of itself is not evil. It is, in fact, of God's design. But the government is designed to serve people and be of benefit to the communities wherein they live. A government that oppresses is a perverse form of government and, therefore, antithetical to the design of God.

The original governmental structure, systems, and culture of the world all had their origins in the creation, as depicted in the first few chapters of Genesis. Of paramount importance is the recognition that the world order, as established by God, was designed to be under the rule and authority of God. Therefore, all authority outside of that original design is outside of God's intent and purpose.

So, what was the Babylonian construct of government, you might ask? The name Babylon has its origins in Genesis, Chapter 11: 1-9. The whole earth was of one language, and the inhabitants at that time determined to come together and build a tower into Heaven and a name that was independent of God. This was an act of rebellion, and God responded by scattering the people all over the earth and confusing their language. Because their language, and therefore their communication among one another, was confused, the Lord called the name of that place Babel, which means *confuse*. This is the origin of the modern-day, saying that someone who is talking but is not making sense is "babbling." This is also the root of the proper noun, Babylon, which means "confusion." Therefore, Babylon is a place of confusion that stems from rebellion to the order of God. So, as we progress through this book, and use the term

"Babylon," keep in mind that this term is synonymous with confusion resulting from disorder brought on by rebellion to God. There have been many "Babylonian" governments and systems on earth recorded in Genesis, and they have always represented a departure from the ways of God.

So, in the days of Daniel, this rebellious King "besieged" God's people to bring them under a rebellious system of government. The word 'besieged' in this verse means "to cramp, to confine, to shut-in, or to enclose." The age-old plan of the Devil is to cramp, confine, shut-in, and enclose the people of God so that they are hindered in their endeavors to worship Him, serve Him, and represent Him in the earth. This was the intent of Nebuchadnezzar.

We must be wise as serpents against the diabolical schemes that come in many forms. While doing so, we must remember that the Bible says that we do not wrestle against flesh and blood but against principalities, rulers of the darkness of the world. Spiritual wickedness cannot be eradicated through natural, earthly strategies. We must lay hold of the mind of God to acquire His spiritual strategies and His supernatural help. The Devil and his team of rebels will not and cannot defeat the purposes of God. Our God is greater, and we are His earthly army, who engage the powers of darkness on behalf of our God. We war through Him, and we win! Amen!

This battle will continue until the Devil is finally, conclusively, and entirely defeated in every way, and Jesus Christ removes him from planet earth and destroys him forever. Until then, we will continue to wrestle with these demonic forces whose work is manifested in things like abortion. It's why we have the wrestling and the fighting about such issues whether it's okay for a baby to be aborted after conception, and whether people are superior or inferior because of their race, or whether we get to choose our sexuality, or whether the earth was created by God or evolved from an atomic or the Big Bang explosion. These and many other issues are simply manifestations of rebellion from God's established order birthed out of spiritual darkness and confusion.

The Kings of Babylon have come to cramp in and take possession of Jerusalem, which is the earthly habitation of the Kingdom of God, with all of its Godly order and values. We have been cramped, we have been confined, we have been vexed, locked out, assaulted in some areas of the world, and some saints have even been put to death. But we are never defeated. Romans 8:37 promises us that we are "more than conquerors through him that loved us."

Many disruptive events are happening in the world today. Presently, we are in the middle of the worst viral pandemic in a century, and it has affected every nation in the world. Furthermore, there have been fires, earthquakes, tsunamis, global warming, strange weather patterns, and a myriad of other maladies of creation that are "shaking" the earth today. The divine plan of God for His earth and humanity is under harsh attack by Babylonian forces.

If you have even a tiny part of your prophetic ears open, you will recognize that something is going on. Everything that can be shaken is shaking. The Bible says the purpose of the shaking is so that everything that needs to be shaken will be shaken so that which cannot be shaken will remain. (Hebrews 12:26,27)

The question that we must ask ourselves is, which category are we in? Are we part that can be shaken, or are we part that cannot be shaken and end up remaining? We each must decide where we will stand spiritually, because in this hour, God is going to shake everything and everybody. Indeed, God is already shaking economies, He's shaking relationships, He's shaking His Church, He is shaking political environments, and He is shaking nations globally.

Now, let's look at Jehoiakim in Daniel 1:1. He was a King of Judah. God had already given a prophetic word to Hezekiah that his Kingdom would not only be shaken, but it would be taken away from him, not while he lived but while his progeny lived. The reason for which we will discover in just a moment.

Daniel 1:2 - "And the Lord gave Jehoiakim King of Judah into his hand..." A lot of times, we think that all the bad things are happening because of the Devil's control. The Devil is not in control. If there is some shaking going on, God permitted it. Even in our own lives, a lot of the shaking that goes on is because the Lord permits it. Sometimes, He allows it because there is something that we need to learn or a skill that we need to acquire, and we will only learn that thing by plowing through an adverse situation and overcoming it.

Also, there are some things about walking in wisdom the people of God need to understand. We need to know that, in some instances, we have ignored the details and suffered because of it. Because of a lack of wisdom, there are many trials and tribulations that we endure that if we had used wisdom, we would never have to go through them. By showing a stranger his precious treasures, Hezekiah did not use wisdom. Because of that, he eventually lost his treasures to the one he allowed to enter his chambers. Daniel 1:2 - "And the Lord *gave* Jehoiakim King of Judah into his hand, with part of the vessels of the house of God: which he carried into the land of Shinar to the house of his god; and he brought the vessels into the treasure house of his god."

There are still times, today, that the Lord will permit modern-day Babylon to take part of our vessels. Sometimes there are doors in our lives and ministries that are carelessly left open, and God will permit us to suffer loss. In these instances, we must pray for wisdom to know what we must correct to redeem our place of dominion. It is a settled fact that Genesis 1:28 is still God's heart for mankind. We have been placed in the earth to establish an earthly outstation of Heaven where we are fruitful, multiply, replenish, have the rule, and exercise dominion over God's creation. That is God's heart for the man and woman that He created. We do that best and correctly when we reestablish and maintain a covenant relationship with Him.

13

Unfortunately, the kingdoms of this world have managed to gain control over all the major governing systems in our time. But we see several instances in the *Old Testament* where kings and rulers who represented the Kingdom of God were able to gain authority over nations and territories for years and years at a time. Men like Joseph, Daniel, David, and Hezekiah were able to change the entire course of nations due to their partnership with God. We must see a resurgence of this kind of dominion in our nations. It is essential that we open our eyes and become aware of things that belong to the Kingdom of God and step up and recapture our rightful positions of rulership.

One key area, for instance, that we must redeem is the institution of the family. We have lost Kingdom authority in the institution of marriage, in keeping fathers with their families, in maintaining healthy family relations, and we're losing our grip on issues of gender identity. God gave them knowledge, wisdom, and understanding of the internal integrity of these matters to His people. Somehow, we lost our grip on maintaining our position of authority in these areas, and the Devil has had a good deal of success in turning the original intent of God into a mess of confusion with devastating consequences.

Marriage is an institution established by God for a man and a woman to come together to love one another, be companions to one another, and create a family through procreation. That institution has been redefined, and the fundamental nature of God's intent in the institution has been distorted by people who have no respect for God's original kingdom purposes or values. We must be proactive in our assignments to redeem the values of the Kingdom of God and determine to develop more *than ten times better* believers.

We have so many promises toward us in the Bible of a victorious life that I often wonder why we see so many Christians living beneath the standard of those promises. God has promised his people "cattle on a thousand hills, that we would be the head and not the tail, that we would be blessed in the house and the field," etc., but so often we see believers who are living so far beneath these promises. I'm convinced that an excellent reason for this is because we have not attended to the conditional aspects of these promises in Deuteronomy, Chapter 28. The conditional "if" statements that begin in verse 1 and pick up again in verse 13 and following are critical to experiencing the goodness of God. So, we have to ask ourselves some honest "why" questions because, in the asking, we will acquire wisdom.

A Mistake Opens a Door for Nebuchadnezzar

Daniel 1:2 says that Nebuchadnezzar carried the treasures of the Lord to his city and put them in the treasure house of his God. This became an opening in the hedge of protection that was previously over the Life of Hezekiah because of his faithful service toward God in making reforms that brought kingdom principles back to God's people. Hezekiah was up to that point an incredible ruler, a dynamic man of God, and an *Old Testament* revivalist. Hezekiah was in the same company as Asa (I Kings 15:11), and Josiah (II Kings 22:2), all of whom did "that which was right in the sight of the Lord." Hezekiah was an incredible reformer, a great man of God, but he made a mistake.

You see, making a mistake is just part of our human existence. We all make them. How many of you can say you've never made one? We all make mistakes. But sometimes, what seems like a small mistake will carry a hefty price tag. You see, we can make a small mistake, and maybe the error only minorly affects our personal life. But then we can make a big mistake, and it affects not only us but also the broader realm of others around us, and even the intents and purposes of God's kingdom.

In this instance, we see that King Hezekiah made a big mistake. He made a mistake that didn't just affect his life and his family; he made a mistake that influenced the kingdom and future generations. What was his mistake? Hezekiah's mistake was trusting a Gentile (unbeliever) King who lied and pretended to be his friend.

We have to be careful about our relationships because the enemy will enter any open door to accomplish his agenda of derailing our purpose. Hezekiah opened the door to unbelievers, who he thought were his friends. How many of us have been wounded by someone that we thought was our friend? This King said to Hezekiah, "You're doing such a good job; let me see what you're doing and how you do it." Sometimes, we think that an enemy is our friend because that person is flattering us. If we are vulnerable to that flattery, we can unconsciously open our lives (and potentially the lives of those we are guiding or caring for) to them and erroneously allow them into our comfort zone, or worse. There are those we may not suspect, that means us no good. They may even be sent by Satan himself to undermine us and even destroy us.

This Babylonian King came to Hezekiah as is recorded in Isaiah 39:1-8 and said, "King Hezekiah, I heard about all the great things you're doing, let me see how you're prospering." King Hezekiah said, "Come on in and see what God has blessed us with. As a matter of fact, look at my house, look at everything I have. Let me take you into the inner chamber and show you some of my private treasure. And look at what we have in the storehouse of the Lord." We must be careful with whom we share our secrets. He shared his secrets, and his inner chambers, with the wrong person. Many years later, we find that Nebuchadnezzar came to Jerusalem and stole the treasures from the house of the Lord and took them to the house of his God, just as the prophet told him that he would.

God told Hezekiah, "Because you did this, you're going to lose your kingdom, and I'm not just going to take it away from you personally, (you're still going to be able to finish out your days as King), but I'm going to take it from your children and your children's children."

Quite often, we fail to understand that our bad behavior is not only affecting us; it is also affecting our children and will affect our children's children. God is not limited by time and generations. He told Israel on multiple occasions, "If you do the right thing, I will bless your generation and the next generation, but if you do the wrong thing, that also will affect as far as ten generations." We must develop a generational mindset as we serve God even in our present generation. What we do does not just impact us personally; it can have good or bad effects on multiple generations.

The Bible says Hezekiah showed one Babylonian King, the treasury of his God. Then a subsequent Babylonian King came back around a few years later and took those precious treasures from the House of Jehovah God. Bringing trouble into your own bosom is worse than trouble coming to you accidentally. But, by God's grace, Hezekiah never lived to see the consequences of his mistake.

Sometimes, we embrace things we have no business embracing and give them access to our lives illegitimately. This is a lack of wisdom. Nebuchadnezzar carried off much treasure from Jerusalem, but the greatest treasures that Nebuchadnezzar carried off were the people of God. The greatest treasure that God has is His people, and His people are being carried off. That's why we have to be very vigilant in the way that we steward the things of God. The greatest treasure that this King stole were the people of God. Daniel was one of those people. Nebuchadnezzar took away the treasures of Hezekiah's house, and he took away God's greatest treasure, His people, and placed them into the house of his god.

Nebuchadnezzar was named after his god, Nebo. Nebo was a Chaldean God who was worshipped and introduced into Assyria. Nebuchadnezzar means "may Nebo protect the crown." His name displayed that he was sold out to his God. Nebuchadnezzar was not trying to be a friend to Hezekiah; he was trying to appease his god.

What happens to leaders who are sold out to their god? In our day, we have Christians who have yet to sell out to their God, but the Devil seems to have no problem getting his people to sell out to him. The Nebuchadnezzars of today have our children, our musicians, our preachers, our prophets, and our marketplace leaders. He's taken what belongs to us, and I don't know about you, but I want mine back. As a son of God walking in the earth, I have an assignment, and part of my assignment is to protect His heritage, and that includes contending for the faith that has been committed to me and my tribe.

We see the great patriarchs of the Bible on assignment to redeem and protect their heritage. We see men like David, Daniel, Paul, and Peter on assignment. We see women like Deborah, Ruth, and Esther on assignment. Likewise, we need to be on assignment for our God today. We need to sell out to our God in a greater measure than the modern-day seed of Babylon is sold out to their gods.

Unfortunately, we often find people of God are intimidated by Babylon, and we erroneously believe that they have greater authority in the earth than we do. It's time to shift the narrative back to the original intent of the government of God.

CHAPTER TWO

PROTECTING
THE KING'S SEED

ONE OF THE MOST PAINFUL THINGS ABOUT READING through the Bible is taking note of the great warfare that the people of God were constantly engaged. Most notably, the warfare of the great men and women of God who contended for the faith in their time and season. From Noah through the Apostles of the first-century church, we find the enemies of God attacking and provoking God's spokespeople. Warfare then is endemic to the assignment of kingdom exploits. Therefore, we cannot see the warfare that we experience as exclusively personal. It really is much bigger than us; it is exclusive to those who are bold enough to embrace God's assignment and determine to remain faithful no matter what.

What we find here in Daniel, Chapter One, is that the Devil is after the King's seed. Let me repeat that we are kings and priests on the earth. According to 1 Peter 2:9, we are a royal priesthood (king-priest) unto God. (Revelation 1:6). We serve a risen King, and we are kings and priests on the earth because of Him. That means that our children are the King's seed. Our children are precious and valuable in the economy of God, and for that reason, the evil does not want them to discover their destinies and certainly doesn't want them to walk in their destinies. So, we must be strong in the Lord and prepared to fight for our inheritance.

This truth is crystal clear in Daniel 1:3, "And the King spake unto Ashpenaz, the master of his eunuchs, that he should bring *certain* of the children of Israel, and of the king's seed, and of the princes…"

The Amplified Bible (2015) translates this verse like this, "And the [Babylonian] king told Ashpenaz, the chief of his officials, to bring in some sons of Israel, including some from the royal family and from the nobles."

You see, the King didn't want just anybody from his captors to serve in his palace; he wanted the best. He wanted those of royal blood and royal breeding. This reminded me of Job 1:6 when Satan appeared before God. He appeared before God and said, "Have you considered your servant Job? He's a faithful believer, but let me touch his life, let me take away his possessions, let me afflict his children and see whether he will still trust you."

God said (paraphrasing here), "Okay. He's in your hands. Go ahead, touch him, I know he's a faithful man." The Devil went out and destroyed all his possessions, tore everything up, and killed his children. Then Satan came back and said, "Hey, God, you know that guy Job? With your permission, I just destroyed everything. What do you think he's going to do?" God said, "He's still faithful." So, Satan said, "Well, he won't be faithful if you touch his body; if you afflict his body, then he'll curse you." And God responded, "Go ahead, touch his body, but you will have to spare his life." Job lost everything but his life and his wife, but he still never cursed God. This is a prime example of the warfare that I spoke of previously. Job lost his children and most of his possessions. The Devil intended to destroy his bloodline utterly; to remove his royal seed. But I want you to know that the story ends with God restoring Job double for all that he lost. God is faithful!

This story is a parallel picture of how the Babylonian Kings came to the people of God with the intent to steal, kill, and destroy. Even Herod tried this when he heard that Jesus Christ was born. But no one can ultimately defeat the ordained purposes of God! Likewise, in the story of Daniel and his trial of imprisonment, he eventually came out victorious because God was with him!

In the context of the Church of Jesus Christ, the Devil wants to enslave everyone, but he is particularly interested in capturing those who are from a royal seed. He wants to steal those with God-ordained intelligence, wisdom, understanding, spiritual insight, creativity, and even people with access to power and lots of money. Ironically, those who were created to serve the King of Kings have great skill sets that the Kingdom of Babylon wants to use for its own agenda. We must proactively resist the Devil when he tries to steal the royal heritage of God and train them to be loyal and faithful to the King of Kings! The King's seed, who is taken from the royal court and used in the counterfeit court, must be redeemed in this hour.

People of God, you are part of the King's seed, and your children are the heritage of the Lord. Commit today to protect your anointing and the anointing of your seed from the contamination of the evil one. How do you do that? By understanding who you are in Christ, learning how to fortify yourself with the Word of the Lord, learning how to walk in the Spirit of the Lord, and by learning how to walk in the Wisdom of God.

Not only does God desire to use His sons and daughters to advance His kingdom, but also the Devil wants to use the King's seed as well. Daniel was a prince in Israel. He was no ordinary guy. If you're a prince, you'd better watch yourself, because the Devil will do anything to pull you away from your destiny. If any princes are reading this, know that the Nebuchadnezzars of the day are after you. The Devil wants to flip you; he wants to change your identity, change your allegiance, and hijack your destiny.

Because of the call that has been on my life from birth, the Devil has been after me all of my life. He has tried to defeat me at every turn. He tried to discourage me, distract me, and destroy me. Before I ever knew who I was, I was a prince. Before I ever planted a church or raised up other leaders for Kingdom service, I was a prince. When the Devil distracted me in college and almost took my life while I was out of alignment with God, I was still a prince. When I was ready to make my commitment to Bible School, the Devil arrived with an opportunity for a promotion. When I was getting ready to plant the church, the Devil came with another promotion distraction. The King's seed is continuously pursued by the enemy to try to distract them, defeat them, and even take their lives.

I'm glad that our King is greater than the gods of this world. I'm glad that I've had angels assigned to me that warred for my life, protected me from harm, and shielded me from destruction even when I was completely unaware of my destiny in God. Maybe you can identify with me, and perhaps you are one of those princes as well.

A few years after I planted the church that I shepherded for almost thirty years, I was still working a full-time job. Someone encouraged me to apply for a job to be a Director of Labor Relations. I applied, had several interviews, and was selected. After several weeks they called me and said, "Hey, you got the job!" My salary was going to increase significantly. I would have entered the six-figure range for the first time. But in my spirit, I knew that I had a bigger assignment in the Kingdom of God. I knew that if I got caught up in that six-figure job, there would be another six-figure job to chase after a few years later. I was in an exceedingly difficult position. I prayed, consulted with a previous supervisor, talked to my wife, and I knew that I had a life-altering decision to make.

Finally, a few days after receiving the offer, I called the department director who had offered me the job and said, "I apologize for leading you astray; I apologize if I put a monkey wrench in this process, but I can't take the job." He said, "Why?" I said, "Because I know my assignment is a full-time ministry, and I know that if I take this job, I'm not going to stay too long, and that would be unfair to you. I must put my assignment with God first.

It was a difficult conversation and a bit embarrassing, I might add, but I had to follow my spiritual destiny. I almost allowed the potential for secular success to derail my spiritual destiny. The King's seeds always have to be aware that they are subjects of spiritual warfare. I had to make the God decision because, at this point, I was an emerging king-priest in the Kingdom of God. I was a King, and Nebuchadnezzar wanted me to serve exclusively in his courts. But my assignment was not to serve in Babylon any longer, God was changing my destiny, and I knew it. The spiritual forces of Babylon put temptation in my path because the enemy of my soul wanted me to abort my spiritual destiny. He wanted me to compromise my call so that God wouldn't get the glory in my ministry. People of God protect your anointing at all costs!

We must determine always to be vigilant. The instruments of Babylon are all around that have an express assignment to steal the resources of God. The text mentions that this King wanted to change the children of God into eunuchs in Daniel 1:3. Eunuchs are specifically assigned to serve in the king's court. Every Babylonian government has eunuchs. They're bright, talented, loyal, ingenious, creative, fiercely loyal. Still, they had their reproductive organs removed so they could not be a threat to the women in the King's court, and it also had the effect of making them more passive by removing their source of potential male aggression.

Even today, the Babylonian-type leadership will endeavor to make neutered eunuchs out of their followers. God never created eunuchs; they are a man-made phenomenon. God formed, made, and created us to be strong and of good courage.

So, the King said, "Bring me the best and the brightest from the Israelite children that we captured. I want those that are princes and the King's seed." Here is the text:

Daniel 1:4, "Children in whom *was* no blemish, but well favored, and skillful in all wisdom, and cunning in knowledge, and understanding science, and such as *had* ability in them to stand in the King's palace, and whom they might teach the learning and the tongue of the Chaldeans."

This King had precise criteria for what he was looking for. Let us take a look at his criteria. The word children referred to youths between the ages of twelve to fourteen. This was an excellent age to indoctrinate bright young youths. The word "blemish" means to have a *stain*, morally or spiritually. Kings have always been a little picky about those who surround them. A moral or spiritual stain would reflect poorly on the king. For instance, these young people could not have a problem with lying, stealing, sexual perversion, or other character defects that would reflect poorly on the king. That would make them unfit for royal service.

Let me interject that what we will be looking at are criteria that a Babylonian King requires for service in his courts. But I would have you to know that the criteria of the King of Kings for service in His courts are much higher. If a Babylonian King demanded such excellence, what must the standard of excellence be for the King of Kings? But we must study these qualifications established by Nebuchadnezzar because it was these standards that Daniel and his friends exceeded. These were legitimate criteria for serving at a high level in Babylon.

Since the fall of Adam, God has always raised up people who could live triumphantly in this world even though they were not of this world, and that is His divine strategy for dominion in the systems of this world. Every standard of excellence utilized by the world is simply a microcosm of the macrocosm of God. God's original intent was for Adam to have access to His divine technology to rule the world. When Adam fell, due to disobedience, he opened the door for a measure of his original authority to be acquired by his fallen prodigy, who has since been governed by the God of this world. But God had a bigger plan; he would send His only begotten Son into the earth to redeem fallen man and empower a whole new race of people with the spirit and nature and authority of the Godhead. That would be us! Praise God! We now have permission, authority, and power to represent the Father, Son, and Holy Spirit in every sphere of the systems of men.

No Blemishes Allowed

The biggest stains the people of God have today aren't the big sins of things like openly worshipping the Devil. No, they are the stains, some big and some small, that compromise their witness. In the marketplace, it is the less than desirable behavior at work that causes someone to disqualify themselves from serving on the Director's key committees (King's court). All things being relatively equal in the marketplace, its most often the small details that separate a successful person from an unsuccessful person except for the unrighteous elements of prejudice and corruption, which are genuine impediments by the way. It's the fine details of practical life skills that separate a person deciding who gets to serve in the King's Palace from one who is excluded.

When I worked in the area of human resources many years ago, I was responsible for conducting the disciplinary hearings for our department. I was often embarrassed and ashamed by the numbers of "devout" Christians who appeared in my hearings for poor behavior, poor performance, continual tardiness, etc. Many seemed to be oblivious to the connection between their work behavior and their proclamation of their faith. On several occasions, when appropriate, I had off-line conversations with these believers to apprise them of the inconsistency of their lifestyles. As Christians, unbelievers will often judge Christians by our behavior, how we conduct ourselves. If we talk one way but behave another, our testimony is destroyed. We must walk the talk if we proclaim the Lord as our Savior.

Some leaders specialize in ministries of deliverance as a means to set people free from blemishes. These ministries certainly have some merit. However, these problems don't usually prevent the saints from serving well in the marketplace. The things that cause even the believer to fail in marketplace dominion are the blemishes that prevent them from serving well. It is most often the blemishes and the stains which are disqualifying them from representing the Lord in critical positions and key places.

Demons do not possess these precious people of God, they are suffering from poor training at home, at school, and at church. They are precious saints who were never educated or trained to know how to rule and reign in the marketplace so that they are qualified to serve in the King's courts. They need to be healed of their blemish through training and development. You may be a son of God, but when you step into higher spheres of service in the kingdom and the marketplace, your blemish will become magnified.

In Biblical times, it was inappropriate to present anything to the King that was blemished. It was disrespectful and dishonorable. In like manner, the sacrificial lamb, who was to be offered to the Lord for the atonement of sin, could not have a blemish. Even Jesus, our Sacrificial Lamb had to be without blemish. Not only does God want those who are blemish-free, so does the Devil. So, remember, if you are sharp, bright, and full of all earthly wisdom, God is not the only one that wants you to serve Him, the King of Babylon does too.

Well Favored

Let's get back to Daniel 1:4, "Children in whom *was* no blemish, but ***well favoured*...**"

The meanings of the Hebrew words well-favored are handsome, good looking, beautiful, pleasing to the eye, of good appearance. A pleasing appearance is necessary for those who will serve in the King's court. A person who dresses well will present a better first impression than the person who is rumpled and unkempt. In some circles, it has become popular to look as unkempt and disheveled as possible. It's become a banner of "cool." But for 99% of those who embrace this lifestyle, it will impede them to serve in King's palaces. It will be difficult for them to sit at the table with decision-makers, with successful people, or with world rulers. They may be brilliant, and sometimes gifted, but because they don't know how to present themselves as well-favored, they will miss out on many vital opportunities.

I'm grateful to my grandmother, who taught me as a young teenager, always to have a good appearance. Dress to the best of your ability, practice good hygiene, behave as if you belong in the room with kings, and never behave poor, even if you are.

I was in Dallas at a conference a few years ago. We did an exercise where I had to look into the eyes of the person sitting next to me. My partner in this exercise was a young lady from Australia. In the exercise, we had to look in the person's eyes and tell them something good that you saw in them. When it came to her turn, she looked at me for what seemed like forever. Then she got tears in her eyes. Finally, she spoke and said, "All I can see in you is majesty and dignity." I was taken aback because this was our first and only meeting. But I understood that not only did she see in the spirit, but also, she was speaking about my appearance and carriage.

Two days later, I was walking through the hall, just going to get a cup of coffee. This lady, who I didn't know, approached me. She said, "Excuse me, sir." I said, "Yes." She said, "I don't know who you are, but there is greatness all over you." Wow! What is that? That's called carrying yourself in such a way that people believe you to be well-favored. People recognize that there is something different about you; something special about you. That is something you carry. There's something about you that people admire and are attracted to. That's well-favored.

Skillful in Wisdom

Let's continue with this record in Daniel. Daniel 1:4, "*Skillful in all wisdom* and cunning in knowledge, understanding science…"

The term 'skillful in all wisdom' is quite interesting. The word 'skillful' is a Hebrew word that means to have insight or the capacity for understanding. This word is also used in Deuteronomy 32:29, "Oh that they were wise, that they *understood* this that they would consider their latter end!" KJV

The words "skillful in all wisdom" occur together, so they must be understood as a single phrase rather than independently. The words "all wisdom" mean "the totality or the entire range of wisdom." Wisdom is the Hebrew word "chakmah." It means the capacity to understand, and so has skill in living. So, putting all of this together, the literal sense of the phrase "skillful in all wisdom" is having the insight and capacity to understand all aspects of skillful living.

As I've said previously, Nebuchadnezzar wanted young men who had demonstrated the capacity to excel in life. He wanted those who had an ability to incorporate knowledge, wisdom, and understanding, not merely in one particular proficiency, but in multiple areas. That's the meaning of skillful in *all* wisdom.

If there is one thing that is sorely lacking in people, young and old, today, it is wisdom. The Kingdom of God needs people like this. But we must intentionally learn how to develop people who are skillful in all wisdom. The king's palace is waiting!

Cunning in Knowledge

The next terms that we must look at in this verse are "cunning in knowledge." Cunning means having dexterity. We would call it being very resourceful. Knowledge has to do with acquiring and possessing information. So, we see another set of qualities that the King was looking for in these Hebrew boys. He was looking for young men who were resourceful in acquiring and possessing information. Resourcefulness is a valuable skill in any profession. Having grown up in both a city environment and a country environment, I learned to be very resourceful. There is no substitute for learning how to get things done, even when you don't have all the pieces immediately at your disposal. Resourceful people save time, money, and materials. Coupled with the ability to acquire, retain, and possess knowledge, a resourceful person becomes a leader amongst their peers. These skills can and should be taught to young people of every age.

In the Body of Christ, we have done a good job of helping people to acquire knowledge, but we haven't done as well in developing people who are resourceful in acquiring and applying knowledge. Generally, we are good at putting people in specific roles or positions and leaving them there for eternity. Even after they have outgrown their assignment, we leave them there. This does a disservice to the person and the ministry. Strategic, apostolic wisdom is needed in developing and placing people in ministry assignments and directing their steps in marketplace assignments. When we master these skills as leaders, we will begin to maximize the people resources that the Lord has apportioned to us.

Understanding Science

The next terms in this verse are "understanding science." The Hebrew word "understanding" in this verse means having the ability to comprehend. It encompasses discernment, perception, and the ability to grasp the meaning of things. The term "science" in this verse means the educational discipline that involves bringing together knowledge, information, and data. In our modern world, these skills would encompass technology, medicine, researchers, pure scientists, etc. Wow! This King is looking for some super bright, gifted, multi-talented young men who would serve in his courts. The better they are, the better his kingship functioned.

Ability to Stand in the Kings Palace

Finally, this Verse concludes with, "…and such as had ability in them to stand in the king's palace, and whom they might teach the learning and the language of the Chaldeans." *The English Standard Version* of the Bible translates this as "competent to stand in the King's Palace." Ability and competence are a bit different in meaning. One can have the ability to build a website, for instance, but not be very competent in doing so. I believe competence is a better interpretation of the meaning of this word because that word is more in sync with the context. This King was pursuing competence, not just ability. So are we those high-level individuals who partner with kings to transform societies and upgrade systems, we must be competent? The Body of Christ certainly needs them to fulfill its assignment. Standing in the King's Palace, as we can see from our study of this verse, is not a passive activity. It is dynamic, transformative, and preeminent in quality.

The term "stand in the King's Palace" is a significant phrase. An applicable definition of this term means [to] stand in front of a superior as an offering, or for evaluation.

This term is used in 1 Samuel 16:22, "And Saul sent to Jesse, saying, Let David, I pray thee, stand before me; for he hath found favour in my sight." KJV

So, we see that standing in the King's palace was no small matter. It was certainly a privilege, but it also carried with its great responsibility. Not just anyone could even enter the King's palace, let alone stand before the presence of the King. I think we take for granted the privilege that it is to stand before men and women of great status and rank naturally and spiritually. God opens the doors to this kind of favor, and when and if we are so privileged, we must take full advantage of it to the glory of God. This wisdom is a significant part of preparing the people of God for ruling and reigning in high places.

The Learning and the Language of the Chaldeans

We finish out this verse and the King's list of desired qualities with this final objective, "Whom they might teach the learning and the tongue of the Chaldeans." The term "learning" represents the entire educational experience of the Chaldeans. That means their gods, their religion, their culture, their customs, etc. These young princes had to be able to completely understand and embrace the way of life of the Chaldeans. The "tongue" represents their language. Anyone serving in the King's palace had to be able to understand the King's language. This included proper expressions as well as figures of speech and other the other cultural nuances of the language of the King and those in the palace.

As we can see, this King was fastidious about how he equipped his royal household and the qualifications for those who had the privilege of serving in the palace. There is much to learn from the standards of this Babylonian King. When we determine to build kingdom sons and daughters in this paradigm, we will then be preparing the people of God to rule and reign with King Jesus Christ in the earth!

CHAPTER THREE

ESTABLISHING A BLEMISH-FREE IDENTITY

D AILY, WE ARE ALL BOMBARDED WITH EXTERNAL STIM-uli that attempt to influence our identity. The community and world events that we are exposed to, the things we consume, the things we read, what we hear, what we see, and our inherent internal makeup, all work together to influence our identity. But we also have an internal identity that is much more influential and dynamic. It's our spiritual nature that comes from our relationship with Christ through the Holy Spirit. In this chapter, we will see how Nebuchadnezzar endeavored to change the identity of his captors by changing their names, their diets, and their external environments. But Daniel and his three friends determined to live from their internal spirit, and it is that dimension that set them apart from their peers.

In Daniel 1:5 we get an insight into Nebuchadnezzar's strategy to change the identity of these sons of Israel. "And the King appointed them a daily provision of the king's meat, and of the wine which he drank: so nourishing them three years, that at the end thereof they might stand before the king."

This King was very strategic in his process of changing the identities of these young men. He knew that to produce the best people, he had to invest the best product. So, he "appointed them a daily provision from the king's meat." But he could only give them the best physical food. He soon discovered that their strength and grace did would not come from the delicacies of the King, but from the spiritual grace of their Heavenly Father.

But this King was committed to replicating a spirit of excellence in his charges. So, rather than feeding them ordinary food fit for servants, he fed them food fit for a king. This wasn't wrong; it was just insufficient for the realm that God had appointed to his servants. The reality is that Babylon can produce greatness, but the greatness that Babylon produces pales by comparison to the greatness of the one true God. Nebuchadnezzar had an elevated standard in his courts from that of the average citizen of his kingdom. But his high standards fell short of the standards in the Kingdom of God. Yet we can learn from the standard that this Gentile King established for his charges. For surely in some instances, the children of this world are wiser in their generation than the children of light. (Luke 16:8) Again, this is a great principle for our learning. If we want to produce kings and priests who will stand with and for our God, we have to feed them with *our* King's meat. Unfortunately, we are often guilty of eating well ourselves, spiritually and naturally, but when we feed others, we feed them with milk, rather than meat. In this generation, the people of God are in desperate need of the meat of God! They have been on milk too long and have become weak and anemic.

I have made it a practice to serve a good portion of meat at every meal. Whether spiritually or naturally, we have been vigilant about making sure that they eat well. We expose them to the best meat apostolically and prophetically. We've recommended conferences to go to, books to read, other ministries to draw from, and introduced them to the best people who we could find who shared our spiritual DNA. Furthermore, in the natural realm, when we have taken them out to eat, we have taken them to the best restaurants we could afford, booked them into the best hotels, and even taken many out shopping to teach them how to buy the best clothes for their money. We have literally practiced these things, and not simply taught them.

I have not always used wisdom in this because sometimes my zeal for the spiritual upgrade of God's people has exceeded their capacity to receive the meal that I've served. But, for those who could receive, their lives have been radically changed, and many of them are doing great exploits for the Kingdom of God. In so many ways, we have been graced to see the fruit of our labor.

So, you see, this Babylonian King was operating in some powerful kingdom principles even though he was not serving the God of the kingdom. Jesus sometimes said the children of the Devil are wiser than the children of God. Let's redeem this principle in our lifetimes and become wiser than the Devil.

These Hebrew princes and "King's seed" were nourished by the King for three years. Three, in the economy of Biblical numerology, is the number of completions. Anything that is done in a set of threes is considered complete. As examples, the Godhead - Father, Son, and Holy Spirit; morning, noon, and night; etc. These young men were nourished for three years with the intent that their entire lives would be transformed from one paradigm to another during that time. The objective was that they would be able to "stand before" the King. That means that they would remain in the presence of the King, to serve him and do his bidding.

We see this principle in operation today in many areas. Take, for instance, our children who we send off to college or military service. In three years or less, they are often radically transformed based upon their diets, their educational exposure, or their training and indoctrination. What if we took the time to invest in the lives of the people of God in a focused way for three years? The objective would be to equip them to stand before King Jesus Christ to wait upon Him, serve Him, and do His bidding? Might we produce more kings and priests to rule and reign in every sphere of culture and society?

As we finish with this verse, let me make a final point. Whatever King we stand before, we must understand that we also are standing before that King's God. Nebuchadnezzar was preparing these sons of Israel to stand before him and before his God. His ultimate aim was to get them to serve his God. He gave them a daily provision, took good care of them, and watched over them every day for three years so they could serve him and his God. For Nebuchadnezzar, this was a progressive system of enslavement. But the one true God had other plans, and his servant Daniel was cooperating with the one true God.

I remember when I was working in a secular position. I was in mid-level management serving in Human Resources, Labor Relations, and as the department's Hearing Officer. I always approached my hearing officer assignment intending to be fair. Because of this, my Director was always sort of disturbed with me because at times I'd rule for the union and other times I'd rule for management. This was because, in my opinion, sometimes, management was wrong, and sometimes the union was wrong. So, I tried to make my decisions for redress based upon what I felt in my spirit was right based upon the facts presented to me.

My director called me in once and said, "Tell me, whose side are you on?" I said to her, "I'm sorry, I'm not on anybody's side. I'm in a position where I'm expected to look at a set of facts and make a righteous decision to give or withhold punishment, and that is what I'm trying to do." She was livid with me. With exasperation, she said, "You need to remember who's writing your check."

She was trying to persuade me to do her bidding, whether it was right or wrong, and I wasn't having it. Her attitude was, I don't care if they are right or wrong, you rule in my favor. She was always working on me, constantly trying to get me to do what she wanted because in her sphere, she was the "King" and I was there to do her bidding. With integrity, I really did try to keep her happy, but at the same time, I needed to be sure that I did not compromise my values.

Standing before a King can be a bit uncomfortable at times as Daniel and his friends would soon discover. After three years of his diet, the King intended that the children of Israel would be ready to serve him. I thank God that when a person grabs hold of the engrafted Word, even Babylon can't talk them out of it. Daniel and his friends were determined to be this kind of believer. Let's take a look at the next verse.

Daniel 1:6, "Now among these were of the children of Judah, Daniel, Hananiah, Mishael, and Azariah." These were the Hebrew names of our principal subjects before Nebuchadnezzar changed their names. All of these young men had a mention of God's Name in their name." Daniel had the "el." El is God. Hananiah and Azariah have the "ah" part of God in their name for Jehovah, and Mishael, again, had the "el" in his name. This is incredibly significant because names were explicitly given to shape identity in the *Old Testament*. Therefore, the identity of these young men was connected to their God. Nebuchadnezzar understood this principle, so one of the first things that he does after receiving these young men into his training program is to change their names. He didn't simply change their names to something meaningless; he changed their names to names that honored the different Gods who he served.

Daniel 1:7, "Unto whom the prince of the eunuchs gave names…"

One of the most fundamental ways to change a person's identity quickly is to change their name. This is a common phenomenon even today when many of our young men and young ladies globally, take on a nickname that identifies them with a street gang, or a cultural community who they want to identify with. This practice is pervasive in specific segments of the entertainment industry. There are even some mystical communities that change the names of their followers to identify with certain spiritual entities that they want to give themselves over to. My advice is to be cautious about what you call yourself because you might just become that personality.

The King of Babylon wasn't simply changing their proper names, he intended to change their identity. Daniel 1:7, "…for he gave unto Daniel the name of Belteshazzar; and to Hananiah, of Shadrach; and to Mishael, of Meshach; and to Azariah, Abed-nego…" He changed all of their names from the name that they received by birth to a name that would identify them with a new god, a new culture, and a new master. He changed the name that reminded them of the God who they served into a name that reminded them of Babylon and its gods.

Today, for instance, if somebody calls you "Little G," or "Old G," and the G represents gangster, you will begin to take on that identity. When you allow someone to call you a gangster, you take on the identity and mentality of a gangster. When you take on the mindset of a gangster, it becomes easier to act like a gangster. It becomes more natural to carry a weapon, and it becomes even more comfortable to use a gun. You have to be careful of what you allow people to call you and how people refer to you. When you begin to identify with a name, even a nickname, it changes your identity; and you begin to think the thoughts of the name that represent you. This is all a ploy of Babylon.

When I was in my freshman year of college, a young lady who I was interested in began to call me Cool Hand Luke. I kind of liked that name, and I liked what that name implied. So, I permitted her and others to call me Cool Hand Luke or Luke for short. After a while, I began to realize that I was starting to act as if I was the coolest cat on campus. I took on an exaggerated persona that went far beyond my natural bent toward "cool." This name and the persona stuck with me throughout my college years, and to this day, some of my old college friends don't remember my name, but they remember my nickname. Alternative names and alternative identities are immensely powerful. Remember, Babylon wants to change your name because when your name is changed, your identity is changed.

Part of the problem with our Kingdom kids is that they endeavor to walk with the Lord but, at the same time, take on the names and personas of Babylon. They are known by nicknames that have nothing to do with the Kingdom. Often times, we permit others to change our name because of deficiencies in our self-image. The new name will often provide a fictional identity that one sees as more significant than their original name and identity. This awareness of a deficiency diminishes our sense of self. It can literally destroy your self-image. It bears repeating that this deficiency would fall into the category of a "blemish."

My deficiency, my blemish when I was in college, was low self-esteem, a need for affirmation, and to be accepted in a group. So, when my friends in school slapped that label Cool Hand Luke on me, I felt accepted and honored and took to it immediately without realizing that it was more like a weight on my back than a badge of honor.

I attended Church throughout my youth, but no one ever recognized my deficiencies and endeavored to minister to them with the Word and the Spirit. No one told me who I was in Christ or looked me in the eye and told me that I was more than a conqueror, or that God would always cause me to triumph through Christ. I was taught religion, but I never came to know the Christ in me. It's for this cause that I am passionate about depositing a ten times better spirit in the minds and hearts of the people of God.

Commitment to God is Intentional

Daniel 1:8, "But Daniel purposed in his heart that he would not defile himself. With the portion of the king's meat, nor with the wine which he drank: therefore, he requested of the Prince of the Eunuchs that he might defile himself."

So, Daniel purposed in his heart that he would not defile himself. Look, we all have to be in the world, but Jesus said you don't have to be of it. Until you purpose in your heart that you will not be defiled, you will be defiled. In this verse, the word "purpose" means to put, place, or set. We need to understand how important it is to put intentionally, place, and set things in our hearts. The heart is the seat of our emotions, our will, and our mentality. In scripture, it represents the whole being of a man, woman, or child (e.g., Proverbs 3:5). Daniel didn't simply mentally decide to refuse the King's diet; he determined in his heart that he would not be defiled by it. There was resolve, commitment, and determination in his decision.

What was it about this diet that caused Daniel to refuse it? Well, the Bible doesn't explicitly say, but we know that Daniel was concerned that he would be defiled by it. The Hebrew meaning of the word defile is to pollute or desecrate. Therefore, we know that there was something about partaking in that diet that would have spiritually or morally polluted or desecrated this prophet of the Lord. My, oh my, what integrity, what demonstration of the character of God. That speaks to something that would compromise his moral or spiritual covenant with his God. What if we could raise a company of saints today, leaders and followers, with this kind of commitment, this kind of fortitude, and this kind of faith? His three friends joined Daniel, and they all requested that they would be exempt from eating the King's meals. God worked on the heart of the man who had to answer to the King regarding their well-being, and he permitted them to eat their preferred diet for ten days (verses 9-14).

The word "heart" is another interesting word. It's not the beating physical heart; it's the inner core of your being. Daniel and his friends decided regarding the inner core of their being. When we get beyond what's politically correct, or what's culturally relevant, and even beyond what is intellectually acceptable, we arrive at the inner core of our heart. What is in the core of your heart? That is what will ultimately be the source of your decisions.

For years and years, I have given myself to the Lord to serve in ministry. Not because it's a lot of fun, I've been in ministry for over forty-five years, and I can honestly tell you that serving the Lord in ministry is not about having fun. There are wars and rumors of wars, challenges more significant than our natural ability to handle, and tests, trials, and temptations that will crush your very being if you fail to maintain your walk with the Lord. Don't get me wrong, there is nothing better than doing something that you know that you've been called by God to do, but just because you are walking in your calling doesn't mean that it's a walk in the park. Daniel was born to walk in this ministry assignment, but it was far from easy, far from fun. It was fulfilling, I'm sure, but being called an "outlier" is never an easy assignment.

For most of my life, I have been an outlier. An outlier is a person who is engaged in a particular assignment but doesn't follow the traditional road to fulfill that assignment. An outlier is usually a pioneer. They have to follow the road less traveled. They must forge a new, often untested path. But God gives them the grace to travel that path that would be impassable for others. I understand that journey. It isn't easy, it isn't pleasant, it can be very lonely, but it is also unavoidable. There is no satisfaction in traveling the traditional road for an outlier. Daniel was such a man. God used him and his friends as a prototype for future outliers, future pioneers, and future kingdom trailblazers. You'll have to be able to endure hardness (2 Timothy 2:3) to finish well, but the prize is worth the journey.

I was having breakfast with a fellow clergyman, and we were talking about ministers and preparing ministers for service. He brought up some great points. He said to me, "You know, young emerging ministers always see the glorious part of the ministry. They like the part of being on stage and ministering the Word of the Lord. But we need to make sure that we share some backside of ministry. Are you familiar with those recruitment ads for the military. You see how they're all crisp and sharp, and they're looking really good? Well, I'm going to get two mannequins. One of the mannequins is going to have one of these sharp guys in a real nice crisp uniform. The other mannequin is going to have blood on him and with a foot blown off or something."

I think that in ministry, we sell the recruitment ad with a nice crisp suit, but we don't show the ones who come back from the battlefield. We don't show the blood on their shirt. We don't show the mental problems that they have. We don't show the difficulties that come from being amid warfare, and therefore people think that ministry is easy. I think that is an accurate assessment. I believe developing ministers need to see both sides.

And so, we see this very thing in the life and ministry of Daniel. Everything was not meant to be easy. We've got to raise some Daniels at this hour. We have to raise up young men and women who know that they are different; know that they are outliers, but they are not afraid to walk in the path of their destiny. Let me speak to our youth. The kids at school may say that you're odd, but they don't understand that you are a Daniel-type person. Yes, you're different, but it's a God kind of different. You are young Daniels in the making who have purposed in your heart that you are going to serve God, no matter what. Many of you, young and old, will have to determine that you don't want the king's diet because the diet that the Lord has prepared for you is better, greater, and in the end, will make you stronger and healthier.

Daniel was full of the fear of the Lord. He was more concerned about what God thought than what the King thought.

He also believed that if he were faithful to God, God would be faithful to him. This is a true example of faith in operation. Daniel could have gone along the path of least resistance and been on the safe side of the path. But he chose to endure hardship if necessary, to be faithful to his God. God saw the faith of Daniel and his friends and responded to their plight with supernatural intervention.

These Hebrew boys said, "Just give us fruits, nuts, and vegetables to eat, and our God will make us fatter, smarter, and wiser than all the other boys who were eating the king's meals." Sometimes we just have to recognize that there are meals, and there are God-given meals. They determined that they wanted to eat the God-given meals. Sometimes you have to be willing to walk away from the spectacular and walk toward the mundane. The pulse that Daniel and company chose was undoubtedly nothing spectacular in the natural. But it was the crème de la crème in the spirit. Daniel obviously knew that a little blandness with the presence of God is better than a grand display of opulence without the presence of God.

As sons of God, we must be willing to eat a meager diet and stay true to our Heavenly Father, even if it means that we will miss out on the flattering foods from Babylon. We must be willing to be an Abraham who offers his only son, believing that even if he gave up his only son that God would make him a father of many nations.

We must have a level of faith that says, "I know that God gave me a prophetic word that I would be a father of many nations, therefore, if God asked me to sacrifice my only son to I will trust him, knowing that he must have another plan." We must believe in His promise so much that we know in your heart that He is going to do something miraculous to keep his promise. We must learn to live on the promises of God, not the promises of men.

Sometimes, our largest blemishes are related to our need for affirmation from those in authority, even those who may not know God. Occasionally, we are tempted to believe in the promises of men that we can see rather than the God who we cannot see. The way that God delivers on His promises are often unconventional to the mind and experience of mankind, but His delivery is always exceedingly abundant in its manifestation. God waited until Abraham was about to sacrifice before He assured him that he would provide His own sacrifice. But it was in that test of character and obedience that God secured Abraham's place as the father of faith and of many nations.

God just needed to see how far Abraham would go. How far are we willing to go to be obedient to the word of God? Are we willing to go all the way? Or will we become fearful and pull back when the going gets tough? We must develop the faith of Abraham, the resolve of Daniel to prove God amid all adversity.

We have many records in the Bible of men and women of God who had to endure many tests of character in their journey of learning to walk with God. On this journey, there are many attempts by Babylon to change your identity, change your diet, change your affections, and change your loyalties. How many young adults have we known who grew up in the church but later allowed Babylon to change their identity?

Accountability is one of the surest ways to maintain fidelity. I remember when I left for college, one of the things that I looked forward to was having no accountability. I wanted to be able to do whatever I wanted to do. And, for four years, that was pretty much the way that I lived. It was in those four years that I literally lost my identity. I thought I was developing my own identity, but because I walked away from ninety percent of my upbringing, I ended up lost. The thing that I desired almost destroyed me. I had grown up in two Christian households; my mother's and my grandmother's. When I went to college, I walked away from Christianity, or so I thought. At least I never went to church during my entire time in college. I was walking in rebellion to what I was brought up in. Everything that I was taught was wrong to do, I did. It was not until I was a senior, near graduation that I woke up.

My grandmother died when I was a college senior, and it shook me to my core. It was then that I realized that I had almost destroyed the foundation she had given me a sense of security in life. I couldn't reconcile my way of life with anything sound, secure, or stable. So, I had to reevaluate the world that I had created and returned to the way of life that provided purpose, peace, and identity. I discovered that living a life without boundaries was a travesty for me. I wish that I had Daniel's fortitude. I wish that I had Daniel's resolve. I wish that I had Daniel's focus and commitment. I could have spared myself many years of hardship and heartache that took me several years of inner healing to recover.

We must resolve to produce Daniel's in this day and hour. When I went off to college, my grandmother and mother were unable to hold me accountable. And, to my recollection, other adults congratulated me on my acceptance to college. Still, no one took the responsibility to follow up with me to ensure that I was staying on the right path. God requires this of His earthly family. We must protect our seed and watch over our inheritance, knowing that there is a world of Babylonian influence that is waiting to capture the princes and king's seed who we have produced.

Therefore, this is why we need to sow the principles of Daniel into the hearts and minds of our young people. They need to know that they are a young prince and princess. They need to know that they are carriers of the seed of God and that future generations will be shaped and developed for God based upon how they structure their lives. This is one of the primary purposes of this book. I want to help redeem the heritage of the Lord. I want to preserve the King's seed that the King of Kings, Jesus Christ, is preparing for Himself.

In many ways, the Church of Jesus Christ, in partnership with parents, needs to recalibrate its training for young people.

They need to be trained to stand before the King of Kings and to serve in his court. They need to know that there are Babylonian Kings who desire to steal their greatness and enslave them in a system that they were never created for. They need to know that the God of Heaven and earth has for-ordained them to represent Him in every high place in the earth. They need to know that they are not attending church just to be obedient children to their parents. They need to know that they are attending church to be trained to reign in life and that the gospel of Jesus Christ will prepare them to do just that.

Let's Change the Narrative

Our churches must become training grounds to produce kings and queens for our God. We cannot see the church as merely a place to feed the poor, or a place to enjoy great fellowship, or even simply a place to gather to worship God. Yes, it's all of that, but it's more. It's a place where kings and queens from Heaven gathered in the earth and to gather other kings and queens who will also be equipped. And they will equip their seed, and their seed's seed. This process will continue from generation to generation until Jesus Christ returns to bring us all together to rule and reign in Heaven and the earth for eternity. This is something that the people of God need to understand in an even greater way because we've made church a religious experience. Then we separate that religious experience from real-life creating a significant disconnect.

What I want to communicate to you is that this environment that we call "coming to church" is not about engaging in religious activity. It's about functioning in a paradigm that God calls "Zoe" [Gk], (life in all of its manifestations). Walking with God is about learning how to live life in all of its manifestations. That's why Jesus said in Matthew 6:33, "But seek ye first the Kingdom of God, and his righteousness, and all these things shall be added unto you." Once we get to the place of seeking God in every aspect of life, our struggles will cease. We must immerse ourselves into the Kingdom of God. This is what Daniel did. He was completely immersed into the King and the Kingdom. This is what we must also do.

When we set the Kingdom of God in our hearts, we become co-laborers with Christ. We become partners with God. We become literally and practically the sons of God - that God. All of us are sons of God positionally, but not everyone is a son practically. Practical sonship takes positional sonship and puts it into action. Daniel purposed in his heart that he would not defile himself because he knew that he was not simply a positional heir of God, but he determined to be a practical heir of God as well. Herein is the difference. Positional sonship without practical sonship produces a religious mentality but leaves us without practical experience. God needs His people to rise up in this day and hour to say, "I'm going to set in my heart that I will not be defiled by Babylon."

Daniel made that decision, and that determined his spiritual destiny from that moment forward. There are moments in everyone's life when we have to make critical decisions that affect our destiny. May we always decide to submit ourselves to God so that we can be instruments in His victorious plan of the ages?

CHAPTER FOUR

DANIEL'S WALK OF FAITH

FOR EVERY GREAT CALL OF GOD, THERE IS A LESSER CALL that will be presented as an alternative. For me, that alternative was always a better job, more money. That was the pattern. When I decided to attend Bible School, I received an offer for a better job. When I decided to plant a church, I received a proposal for a better job. After I planted the church and was preparing to go into full-time ministry, I received an offer for a better job. This means someone other than God was watching me and endeavoring to throw me off course. The question before me was always, *Do I turn toward the money, or do I turn toward God?* So far, I've always turned in the right direction, and God has never failed to supply my needs according to His riches and in His glory.

We are always in a battle with the forces of Babylon. The Bible, in Ephesians 6:12, calls them principalities, powers, rulers of the darkness of this world, and spiritual wickedness in high places. These spiritual forces are behind the Babylonian culture of our day. Make no mistake about it, there are spiritual forces at work for us and with us, and there are spiritual forces at work against us. The Word of the Lord assures us that we are "more than conquerors" in all these things (Romans 8:37). But Ephesians 6:12 reminds us that we are in a wrestling match.

I have been and continue to be engaged in the wrestling match, and so have you. What these malevolent forces, led by the God of this world, wants to do is to steal, kill, and destroy us. They are after our person, our families, our callings, and our destinies. The weapons used against us will vary. All of us have strengths that are our defense, and we have weaknesses that are holes in our armor of defense. I grew up in poverty, so one of the weaknesses that I had to be aware of was the desire for money that would be a defense against the poverty I experienced as a child. I have always endeavored to be mindful of my weakness in this area, so the Devil, in whatever form he may appear, will not be able to take advantage of me.

The Bible says that there are four categories of how people receive the Word of God when they hear it (Mark 4:3-8). Three of these ways are ultimately unprofitable. The four categories are:

1. Those who hear the word, but it falls by the wayside;
2. Those who hear the word, but it falls on stony ground;

3. Those who hear the word, but it falls among thorns; and
4. Those who hear the word, and it falls on good ground and bears fruit.

These four categories are very real and will determine the fruitfulness of the Word of God in the life of everyone who hears it. Each of us individually and personally decide which category we fall in based upon the decisions that we make when challenges come our way. We all will have the stony ground challenge, the wayside challenge, the thorn challenge, and the good ground opportunity. These challenges and opportunities test our character and test our will and our resolve. Daniel and his friends were each being tested. Their decision to stand for and with God was the difference between being a category one through three, or a category four life.

These are what I call life's defining moments. There are very definitive moments in everybody's life. It doesn't matter who you are; you're going to have some defining moments. These moments may come in our marriage, our ministry, our job, or our spiritual life, but we'll all have defining moments. The decisions we make in those defining moments will determine our destiny. What we purpose to do in those defining moments will determine our destiny.

Daniel's decision not to eat the King's meat catapulted him into a walk of faith with God that he had not previously known. What if he had decided that he was going to eat the King's meat? He would not be one of the patriarchs of the Bible. His story would have never been known universally by everyone who reads the Bible. He would have never gained a good reward in the courts of heaven. He would have never been listed in Hebrews 11 with the men and women of great faith.

There are defining decisions that we all have to make, and oftentimes, we are confronted with those decisions amid a crisis. There are decisions that you and I will have to make that will determine whether we step into a greater realm of experiencing God, or whether we simply live mediocre lives of comfort and safety.

Daniel moved from a life of mediocrity as a slave, into a dynamic life of conquest and exploits as a man of faith. Why? Because he decided to walk on the high road with God rather than the road of comfort with men. He took a risk to walk with God when his very life was on the line. How many times have you been faced with a life-changing decision? Did you make your decision based upon fear or faith? Daniel chose faith, and that decision made all the difference in his life and destiny.

Daniel and his three friends decided they were not going to eat the King's meat. Ask yourself these questions:

- *Are there some decisions that I'm in the midst of making right now?*

- *What will my future in God be like based upon the decision that I am making today?*

This is really where the rubber meets the road. He decided based upon faith. He heard God say that he was not supposed to defile himself. So, he made the decision not to defile himself. Daniel demonstrates that we can choose to be comfortable and safe and live a life of mediocrity, or we can choose to take the risk of going out on edge with God, catapulting ourselves into a whole new dimension of a walk of faith.

In Daniel, we able to see an example of the fear of the Lord. He literally feared God more than he feared man. If he didn't have a fear of the Lord, he never would have never made those decisions.

The story of Daniel reminds me of other faith heroes listed in Hebrews 11. In verses 33-34 in the Chapter of Hebrews, God refers to Daniel and others that walked in great faith with this declaration:

> Verse 33 - "Who through faith subdued kingdoms, wrought righteousness, obtained promises, stopped the mouths of lions,

> Verse 34 - "Quenched the violence of fire, escaped the edge of the sword, out of weakness were made strong, waxed valiant in fight, turned to fight the armies of the aliens."

Faith has many footprints, but they all lead back to God. When Abraham ascended the mountain to present his son as a burnt offering to the Lord (Genesis 22:1-ff), he stepped out in faith according to the Word of the Lord that he had heard. He literally said, "God will provide Himself a lamb for a burnt offering." Abraham simply put one foot in front of the other and continued to move toward the promise of God, even though there was no physical evidence that a physical offering was available. Paul described Abraham's faith as "against hope [he] believed in hope" (Romans 4:18). True faith moves in an atmosphere of natural impossibility and improbability. So just as Abraham climbed the mountain prepared to offer a lamb for a sacrifice, even though he had no lamb, Daniel believed that God would take care of their physical bodies even though they were barely eating any food. Indeed, God honors faith that is as a grain of mustard seed.

In Daniel 1:9, we see that this is going to start working in Daniel's favor to ensure that Daniel is not dishonored due to his faith. "Now God had brought Daniel into favor and tender love with the prince of the eunuchs."

In the course of our walk with God, He will give us divine favor with people and cause us to be attracted to them and them to us, for no apparent reason. The Bible says that this Prince of the Eunuchs had a favorable love and tender love toward Daniel. This favorable love helped to determine the destiny of Daniel and his friends. We have to know when God is giving us favor and then have the wisdom to move in that direction. Sometimes, there are people in Babylon who God will cause to be favorable to us. This guy wasn't a believer in the God of the

Hebrews, but God was going to use him to help Daniel out. Sometimes, God is moving amid our circumstances and will use someone who is not a fellow believer to be a blessing to us. This is one of the reasons that we are encouraged to demonstrate the love of God toward everyone. We really never know who God will use next to advance His Kingdom.

Shortly after I graduated from college, I worked a job with a man who was a stark unbeliever. He told me that he was an agnostic. We had many discussions about the gospel of Christ, but I was never able to convince him to become a believer (as far as I know). But this man was exceedingly kind to me. He mentored me well and did everything that he could to ensure that I was successful.

After leaving that job, I moved to Washington D.C., and my supervisor was also a non-Christian. As a matter of fact, she was a practicing Buddhist, and we also had many discussions about religion and the gospel of Christ. Again, we were respectful in our conversations and never spoke disparagingly of one another's faith. She also was truly kind to me. She recognized my talent, appreciated my ability, and was pleased with my work. She also became an extraordinarily strong mentor to me in my secular capacity, and I was promoted and given cash awards under her tutelage. In both of these situations, God used someone who was an "unbeliever" to be a blessing in my life and to assist Him in moving me toward my ultimate destiny. Each of these individuals respected God at work in me, even though they were not acquainted with Him. As followers of the Lord Jesus Christ, we must make sure that our attitude toward the unsaved is not demeaning or off-putting in any way. God is on the throne as we say, and He is at work throughout the universe to ensure that we are more than conquerors in all things.

You see, sometimes, as Christians, we get mad at the gatekeeper when the gatekeeper is simply doing his job to maintain the gate. He's really just following orders but has the freedom to dispense grace, when and if he so chooses. We must become better at being hospitable and extending grace and long-suffering to those who are simply functioning in a Babylonian system. Many times are unaware of the larger picture. Sometimes we get distracted into fighting with the gatekeeper and forget that we don't wrestle against flesh and blood but against principalities, and powers, etc. So, if God gives you favor with the Prince over the Eunuchs, take the favor. You may need it to get out of prison one day.

There is so much wisdom and revelatory principles woven into this record in Chapter 1 of Daniel. In Daniel 1:10, the word of the Lord says, "And the prince of the eunuchs said unto Daniel, I fear my Lord the King, who hath appointed your meat and your drink: for why should he see your faces worse liking than the children which *are* of your sort? then shall ye make *me* endanger my head to the king."

There are a lot of people captivated by Babylon, who are just as disturbed as you are about Babylon. A lot of people in Babylon are looking for a Daniel to show them how to get out of Babylon. This man is very being very honest. He's saying, "Why should I buck the system and let you eat something that the King has already told me not to let you eat?" We must be sensitive to people who are entrapped in a system, and to date, they have been unable to get released. They aren't the enemy; they just work for the enemy.

Verses 11-13 of Daniel tell us, "Then said Daniel to Melzar, whom the prince of the eunuchs had set over Daniel, Hanahiah, Mishael, Azariah. Prove thy servants, I beseech thee, ten days; and let them give us pulse to eat, and water to drink. Then let our countenances be looked upon before thee, and the countenance of the children that eat of the portion of the king's meat: and as thou seest, deal with thy servants."

Wow! What a declaration of faith! Daniel said, "Put us to the test for ten days! Do you have the faith to prove God?" I want to tell you that there are webs, and traps, and prisons that we all find ourselves in from time to time that we will never break when we are afraid to trust God implicitly. Daniel was very bold in proclaiming his faith. He said, "Prove thy servants for ten days." Hebrews 11:6 says, "But without faith, it is impossible to please him: for he that cometh to God must believe that he is, and that he is a rewarder of them that diligently seek him" (KJV).

One of the major aspects of walking in faith toward God is that we must believe that He is a rewarder of those who seek Him! Daniel said, "Put us to the test." He said that because he was already convinced that his God was able to take care of him. He was convinced that God was a rewarder of those who diligently seek him. Daniel was not a passive believer; he was a diligent believer. He followed the laws of God; he trusted God; he was fully persuaded about his God.

Daniel knew what was at stake. His very life and the life of others were on the line. But amid that pressure, he still stood his ground and said, "Prove us! The walk of faith requires boldness. One has to be fully persuaded and confident in the God they serve."

On several occasions in my life, I have stepped out in this way and essentially said, "Prove us!" When I entered Bible School, I emptied my retirement account, sold a brand-new car, and put all of our monies into tuition to attend. We were a young family of three, and before we graduated, we were a family of four. My retirement funds and all of our savings barely covered the first six months of school. With no loans and no savings, we graduated four years later with no debt. God, in His sovereignty, provided our every need. Let me be clear; we had some awfully close calls, but God never failed to come through for us, and oftentimes, it was in the last hour. Someone always came through at the right time and place.

On one occasion, there was a young man who served in the ministry with us who asked in passing how current we were on tuition. I told him that we were in dire need of a donation because our next payment was due in a few weeks, and we had nothing to contribute. He said that he had money in an investment account that he had not looked at for quite some time. He said that he would get back to me in a couple of weeks after checking his account. When he returned to check back with me, he said that he had withdrawn the money and closed the account. He asked how much our tuition payment was. I told him, and he looked at me with shock on his face. He then handed me a check that was for the exact amount that we needed, to the dollar. We both rejoiced in the faithfulness of God. I have learned that our God delights in supplying the needs of His people. He is, after all, El Shaddai; God Almighty!

I know Daniel must have had a conversation in his natural mind that went something like this. I know this doesn't make sense for me to defy the King. I know it doesn't make sense for me to refuse His meat and go on a 10-day pulse fast, but I believe that God will reward me for being faithful to Him.

The walk of faith can be a very tricky process. Many times it requires the willingness to take significant risks. But upon hearing the Word of the Lord either audibly or as an inner witness spiritually, it is incumbent upon us to step out in faith. This is how you walk in faith with God.

Daniel said, "Give us just ten days, and I believe that in ten days, God will show up." I believe the spirit of the Lord rose up in this man, and he started on a journey for which there was no turning around. This is the journey of faith. May we consider whether we have become too comfortable in Babylon? When all of your needs are supplied in Babylon, what would be the need to believe God? What would be the need to walk in faith? In our modern cultures, have we created environments where the government supplies all of our needs, by your job, by charitable organizations, by benevolent churches, etc.? Particularly in what is known as first-world societies, have we removed the incentives for even the people of God to trust God, to believe God, to have faith toward God? If we don't have something that we need, we turn to a charitable organization to see if they will supply it. Make no mistake, I believe that charitable organizations are great, but sometimes, I believe that they become a replacement for us to believe God. And that is a huge spiritual problem.

May it be known in the communities of the saints that the faith walk is a training ground for a dynamic walk with God. Faith was a training ground for Abel, Enoch, Noah, Abraham, Sarah, and numerous other biblical patriarchs, including Daniel (Hebrews 11:4-ff). God said in Hebrews 11:6 "...that without faith it is impossible to please God." Faith then must be taught, modeled, spoken of, and lived out in the community of the saints. Let's return to the experience and the exploits of faith that were the norm for patriarchs of old.

Ten Days of Testing

Daniel 1:14-15, "So he consented to them in this matter, and proved them in ten days. And at the end of ten days their countenances appeared fairer and fatter in flesh than all the children which did eat the portion of the king's meat."

Daniel requested that they be permitted to eat pulse for ten days, and then they could be compared with the other captives who were eating from the king's dietary plan. This request was granted. At the end of the ten days, they were examined and found to be fairer and fatter in the flesh than all the children that ate of the King's meat. Praise God, Daniel and his friends stepped out in faith, and God did not allow them to be put to shame or to be disappointed. I want to ask you a question. When was the last time that you stepped out of your comfort zone to prove something to God? Malachi 3:10 says, in part, "Prove me now herewith saith the Lord of Hosts."

God loves to be put to the test. He loves for His people to step out on His promises and allow Him to show Himself strong on our behalf. God showed up for Daniel and his three friends. They asked to be allowed to prove there was a God, and God showed Himself to be faithful.

This is an example for us to follow in learning how-to walk-in faith toward God. Remember, every crisis is just an opportunity for us to believe God. And also know that every miracle that was ever manifested, had a crisis that preceded it. You don't prove there is a God when everything's going great; when all of your needs are met, and you're living on top of the world. Faith is birthed amid crises. We don't have to believe God for the crisis to come; crises are birthed on the battlefield of life. Crises are birthed in the divine tug of war between thy Kingdom come (a request based upon a promise), and thy will be done (the manifestation of the promise). But when the crisis comes, be ready with the weapon of faith to wage war against the enemies of your destiny!

Can you imagine the faces of the King's guards when those Princes of Israel stepped up to be examined, and they were in better shape on their God-diet than the others were on the King's diet? In the natural, it just doesn't add up. It doesn't make sense in the natural order of things. Let it be known that when we step out to prove God, it will often make no sense to the established order of things. But God is not restricted to man's order of things, nor is He limited to the natural laws of our world. Walking with God provides an opportunity for us to experience the supernatural dimension of God, who supersedes the natural realm. What a privilege!

I want to share another miracle with you from our personal story. During our Bible School days, my wife was pregnant with our second daughter. It was during our year "on the field." (A time of proving God based upon what we were trained to do in residence). We were in Detroit, Michigan. I was working, but the job I had did not have benefits. My wife was working as a waitress, so she had no benefits either. After about five or six months, we decided that we needed to find an obstetrician who could prepare her for the birth, and perhaps we could find one who would permit us to establish a payment plan. We prayed about it and asked God to show us favor in the process.

I don't remember how, but we did find a doctor, one of the leading obstetricians in the state of Michigan. He was very gracious and kind to us and gave my wife the best of care during her final months of pregnancy while permitting us to pay just pennies on the dollar out of pocket. In the final weeks before labor and delivery, during one of her visits, the doctor told my wife that he knew that we had no insurance to have the baby in the hospital through normal channels, so he said that he would deliver our baby at no charge. He instructed her that when she went into labor, she should call him, then met him at the hospital, and he would take care of everything from there.

That is exactly what happened; another miracle in this miracle. When we arrived at the hospital, we discovered that our daughter was in a breached position in the womb, and he was the only doctor in the state who knew how to turn a breached baby in the womb to prepare it for birth. Mother and daughter had an uneventful birthing process, and my wife and baby were back home the next day. I want you to know that God is faithful, and He loves to show Himself strong for His people. So get in the habit of proving God. Put him to the test and let him show Himself strong in your situation.

Fatter and Wiser

Daniel 1:16-17, "Thus Melzar took away the portion of their meat, and the wine that they should drink; and gave them pulse.

As for these four children, God gave them knowledge and skill in all learning and wisdom: and Daniel had understanding in all visions and dreams."

Wow! Isn't this just like our God? Not only were "these four children" fairer and fatter than their peers, but God gave them a few extra bonuses in the package. He gave them "knowledge, and skill in all learning, and wisdom, and understanding. Guess what? That is exactly what the King was looking for, except God provided these qualities to these servants in abundance and on another level. This is very critically important for us to understand. In a subsequent chapter, we will address this subject in more depth, but for now, let me mention that here we have mention of three of the seven spirits of God: knowledge, wisdom, and understanding. Isaiah, Chapter 11:2 lists all seven of them as resting upon Jesus Christ.

Daniel and company asked simply to be permitted to eat in such a manner as not to defile their God. What they received, in turn, was permission to do just that, but in addition to that, God birthed something else in them who was of heavenly origin. He gave them three of the seven spirits of God, plus skill in all learning.

This story gives us great insight into the ways of God. There is a greater revelation that opens up to you on the other side of that critical decision you have to make, on the other side of that challenge that you are faced with, and on the other side with your decision to go with God at any cost. Not only are your needs supplied, and you're fairer and fatter, but a spiritual DNA is birthed in you. Three of the seven spirits of God were birthed in them, and this was just the beginning.

What is waiting to be birthed in you? What has not come into manifestation yet because you have not made a critical decision at a crucial time? Do you think God is going to unlock the seven spirits of God in you while you sit in joyful repose or passive bliss? I don't think so. These experiences happen at overly critical times in your life when your back is against the wall, and you have to make a decision that may not make sense and may not be pleasant. Do you have the courage to make the unpopular critical decision at an unpleasant moment? You must know that on the other side of those kinds of decisions, your needs will be supplied according to His riches and glory and there's an anointing that's going to be birthed that God didn't even tell you about.

They never asked God for knowledge, wisdom, and understanding. But God gave that to them as a bonus. We need to continually be reminded that we can never out-give God! He will always go exceedingly abundantly beyond to repay in a manner of sacrifice that we have given to Him. God wants to supply all of your needs according to His riches in glory, and then He wants to go beyond your need and give you more than you asked for. That's just His way.

When I made the decision and the sacrifice to go into Bible School, I didn't have very much in the way of material things during those four years, but man, oh man, did I step into the training school of God in a whole new way. I received in the spirit realm much more than I ever paid for in the natural realm. Before then, I didn't know very much about walking in faith or the practical aspects of spiritual warfare or dealing with demonic spirits in people of communities. I learned all of that and more because I was willing to sacrifice my career and my finances to pursue a deeper walk with God.

While I was working in Washington, D.C., in my comfortable job, enjoying my comfortable salary and working for the Lord as much as I comfortably could, I was only scratching the surface of my spiritual potential.

I've mentioned my interim year assignment during my Bible School years. In the natural, it was one of the toughest years of my life. But spiritually, it was one of the greatest. One of the jobs that I worked was as a youth counselor in an intervention program for troubled youth. These were youths who the traditional school system had given up on. I was able to minister to a seventeen-year-old girl who was caught up in prostitution since she was thirteen. I was able to minister salvation to her and then to cast out spirits of perversion and fear. She became a new creation right before my eyes.

I ministered to a young man who had multiple "personalities" inside of him who would all speak in different voices. You could pass by his door and hear conversations of what seemed to be five or six different people. Everyone was afraid of him, but he permitted me to work with him, and he learned to trust me without fear. Every month, I'd put him in my car, and we'd go for a drive so that he could use his clothing allowance, and I never had an incident with him. Others, on the other hand, would end up having some kind of altercation with him, so no one wanted him on their caseload. God gave me favor with him, and I was able to help him when no one else could or would. I learned how to minister deliverance, healing, salvation, and restoration in multiple ways on just that one assignment.

Had I not made that decision in Washington, D.C., to leave my comfortable job for an uncomfortable assignment in my pursuit of more of God. I would have never been able to grow up in my walk with God. Sure, I would have had a great job, many promotions, a comfortable lifestyle, maybe good health, but I would have no real cutting-edge experience in walking with a supernatural God.

So that is why I've always taught that experiential anointing is birthed in crisis. The experiential anointing is not birthed in comfort. Many of you may be waiting for God to do something supernatural in your life, but you're not willing to be uncomfortable enough to allow Him to be your hero.

Jesus trained his disciples in lectures, everyday encounters, and on-the-job experience with real-life issues. They dealt with crises of sickness, crises of persecution, dilemmas of death, crises of demonic encounters, crises of weather, and in all these things, he demonstrated the supernatural power and authority of God to overcome every situation. This is the way of Jesus; it's the way of Daniel; it's the way of Moses; it's the way of Abraham, and it's the way of God.

I long to see the church get back to that kind of faith, that kind of courage, that kind of daring, that kind of walk of faith. Getting back to our record in Daniel, Chapter 1, the text says that God gave them knowledge, wisdom, understanding, and the ability to understand all learning.

Daniel 1:18, "Now at the end of the days that the King had said he should bring them in, then the prince of the eunuchs brought them in before Nebuchadnezzar."

Daniel 1:19, "And the King communed with them; and among them, all was found none like Daniel, Hananiah, Mishael, and Azariah: therefore stood they before the king."

The training program for these young princes and King's seed lasted approximately three years. It was now time to appear before the King, and the text tells us that among them all, there were none found like Daniel, Hananiah, Mishael, and Azariah. Notice here that the scriptures use their Hebrew names, not their Chaldean names. They remained true to their God. They kept their true identity. They remained true to their diet; they kept the spirit of their worship pure before the God of Heaven and earth.

Furthermore, the text says that after the King conversed with them, he found no others who could measure up to these four. This testimony had nothing to do with their political connections, nothing to do with their financial contributions, nothing to do with their status in society; it had everything to do with their relationship with their God. God saw a reflection of Himself in them and therefore promoted them above their peers.

May it be so with us, may we raise the seed in the earth that looks like Daniel and Hananiah, Mishael, and Azariah!

CHAPTER FIVE

THE REALM OF TEN TIMES BETTER

"And in all matters of wisdom and understanding, that the King inquired of them, he found them ten times better than all the magicians and astrologers that were in all his realm."

DANIEL 1:20 (KJV)

D ANIEL AND HIS THREE FRIENDS' NAMES WERE CHANGED by Nebuchadnezzar, but he could not change their hearts. Standing firm on their faith, they maintained their fidelity to the God of Heaven and earth. They didn't do it for earthly promotion; they did it for fame or fortune; they did it for God. God rewards those who diligently seek Him, and their first reward was to stand before the King and be acknowledged as better than all of their peers. God assures us that any labor for Him is not in vain. Daniel and his friends are proof of that principle.

After maintaining their diet and refusing to bow to the idolatrous edicts of their captor, these Hebrew sons received from God wisdom, understanding, knowledge, and the ability to excel in the language and the learning of the Chaldeans. This is the bonus package that God gave them for their faithfulness to Him. It was not the diet that made them fatter and leaner, and their appearance and countenance stood out to the King. It was the intangible bonuses that God added to the mix that made the difference. It was the activation of supernatural grace that catapulted them above and beyond their peers. There is no mention from the King of the other physical attributes, much of which they already possessed. The things that stood out to the King were the things that were birthed in the spirit realm.

These are the things my friend, which will make a difference in our lives. When God adds His measure to our natural gifts, talents, and abilities, that's when we excel among our peers. Better, is a comparative term indicating that something or someone is exceptional beyond the norm. God is an exceptional God, and He produces exceptional fruit. Because we are made in His image and likeness, we are also wired to be exceptional people.

Several years ago, I did a series of messages on this topic in our local church. After depositing these principles into the hearts of our people, I started a mentoring program called "10 Times Better" for our junior high and high school-age youth. It was an absolute delight to watch those young people who were the King's seed and princes excel spiritually and academically. It is a fact that we never had a high school dropout during our program. We taught them the Word of the Lord; we taught them decorum; we taught them how to tap into their unique and God-given graces. All of our young people finished high school, and either went to college, trade school or military afterward. Many of them excelled above their peers and received full package scholarships. Many of our youth credit the mentoring experience with inspiring them to excel on another level. We must intentionally invest in God's heritage in a more considerable measure. If we don't develop them for the kingdom, Babylon will steal them.

When your child stands before the King of Babylon, what is he saying about them? Is he saying that they are average and mediocre, or that they are ten times better? Do they just stand before the King, or do they stand out?

As I mentioned, *ten times better* is a superlative phrase. God often speaks in superlative language when He is talking about us. Let's pause and reflect upon some superlative language that God uses when He is speaking about us:

- We are made in His image and His likeness. Genesis 1:26
- We are fearfully and wonderfully made. Psalm 139:14
- We are his royal priesthood. 1 Peter 2:9
- We are the light of the world. Matthew 5:12

- We are equipped to do greater works than Jesus. John 14:12
- He abounded toward us in all wisdom. Ephesians 1:8
- He wants to show us great favor. Ephesians 2:7

The world ought to see us and know that because of Christ, we are ten times better. In the classroom, in the boardroom, on our jobs, in sports, in the arts. We have a competitive advantage, spiritually, if we choose to use it.

The King compared Daniel and his friends with his magicians and astrologers. The word magicians describe one who was a diviner, one who practiced secret arts, and others were keepers of the books that contained the knowledge of secret things. Some believe that these were the predecessors of the "wise men," the Magi, which came looking for Jesus at his birth. They were skilled scribes and ones who could interpret the language of the stars. These men were very educated and spent their lifetimes perfecting their craft. But Daniel and his friends stood head and shoulders above them all.

Likewise, the astrologers were the occult artists of their day. They were those who specialized in the occult arts and communication with the dead. These were familiar practitioners in the dark side of supernatural activity. But Daniel had a greater connection with the superior source of supernatural power, the almighty God.

It should be said of us today that we are ten times better than the astrologers, than the magicians, than the mind readers, than the fortune tellers, than the palm readers, than the shamans, than the witch doctors, and the warlocks, and the Satanists of our day. But we must have the will and the faith to walk a different path. We must be ready and willing to trust God and to walk with Him on another level.

Today we see a lot of magic and seduction and mind manipulation on an entirely different level. We have taken the magical arts and folded them into advertising and used them to manipulate people and distribute misinformation. The political realms, economic realms, religious realms, and entertainment realms are full of magic and seduction. They know how to frame it. They know how to market it. They know how to put it all together to seduce the multitudes. The time is ripe for a new day Daniels. We must raise up a new generation of Daniels who are better than all the magicians, shamans, and soothsayers. We need to raise up a generation of Daniels who can demonstrate that one can achieve success in any discipline by walking in integrity and in the spiritual technology of the preeminent God of the universe.

We are walking in this realm of *ten times better* when we decide to step over into the supernatural of God, to step over into the provision of God, to get out of a comfort zone and say, "God, I want to prove you, I want to put you to the test." There are decisions that we have to make, much like Daniel did. We have to purpose in our hearts that walking with God is the greatest value in life. On the other side of that, is a supernatural realm of grace that we will never discover until we take that step. God is looking for people with Daniel's heart and spirit who are willing to prove Him.

True Intercessors

Daniel did not go on this journey alone. Three other intercessors went with him - Shadrach, Meshach, and Abed-nego. An intercessor is someone who has a prayer meeting with God on behalf of someone else. Daniel said, "Hey, guys, come pray with me because we need a miracle." God did a miracle, but that was just the beginning. Even later on, when the King said that no one could pray to any other God, Shadrach, Meshach, and Abed-nego joined Daniel in praying to their God three times a day. I'm sure that some people were saying, "Didn't we tell you not to pray to your God? There's a law that says if you pray to your God, your punishment is death." But they did not care. They remembered the God who had delivered them before and were confident that He would deliver them again.

Nebuchadnezzar was so impressed with Daniel and his friends who he promoted them to high positions of authority in his Babylonian government. But Nebuchadnezzar did not know Daniel's God. Many of you have been, and many more will be, promoted in the Babylonian structures of society. But when you are promoted, you can't become a Babylonian. You can't succumb to your environment. You will need to maintain your focus and your fidelity and prove that the God who you serve is higher and greater than any obstacle or circumstance that you encounter.

In the upcoming verses, we will see King Darius come into an understanding and relationship with Daniel's God. Daniel was promoted and was exercising great authority in dominion in the land of the Babylonians, even though the kings that he served were not fellow believers in Daniel's God.

Now, I touch on this because as many of you endeavor to ascend a mountain, whether it be a mountain of education, a mountain of business, a mountain of family, or a mountain of government, we'll still have somebody over you who is a Nebuchadnezzar. As a matter of fact, much of your journey will be like that. We all need to remember that even though we are amid Babylon, we can still rule in the middle of our enemies, as is declared in Psalm 110:2.

Sometimes, we get the mistaken impression that the only place and the only time we can exercise authority is when everyone is a believer. No! God wants us to be able to triumph through Christ, no matter where we are. Daniel demonstrated that a sold-out believer of the one true God, can be amid Babylon and still exercise God-ordained dominion.

We want to take our princes and princesses and train them up to be in Babylon, but not of Babylon. We want to take these intelligent young people and make sure that their intelligence is molded and constructed under the anointing of the Holy Spirit to such a degree that they can walk in and amongst Babylon yet not be touched by Babylon. The problem that we have with many of our young people, even when we trained them in the Word of the Lord and send them to Christian schools, is that after they get out from under our umbrella, they don't know how to remain true to their God even while being amid Babylon. We have to change that.

You see, post-high school and college are usually where we lose most of our seed. It's after high school that they enter into the Babylonian realm. This is where they will have to decide about whose diet they will be fed with. It's interesting to note that as young teenagers at the time of their captivity, these young men did not have the benefit of their parent's "covering" as it were. They were on their own. It was them and God, and the world of Babylonia that they had been brought into. So at the tender age of let's say seventeen years of age, give or take a few years, they had to be mature enough and have enough of the word of the Lord and the spirit of the Lord inside of them that they can make a decision to follow their God rather than a foreign God.

We've seen all these principles in the first chapter of Daniel. In Daniel Chapter 2:1, we have Hebrew children who have already become recognized as being ones who are from a whole different order.

We see God laying the foundation in this book of Daniel for a different order of people. God took a group of young men who were intelligent and spiritually connected to God and caused them to be raised up in a hostile environment but eventually becoming respected rulers in that government. God took a man like Daniel, who was a young Prophet, and taught him not only how to be a Prophet in a foreign land but also how to be a King in that land. So he's a Prophet, and he is serving as a king. He literally becomes Vice President in the kingdom. The Bible says that Darius promoted Daniel to a status similar to our Vice President, or Prime Minister. So he was a functional King in Babylon.

As you read these words right now, you might realize that you are in Babylon yourself. Every Monday, you go to work in a Babylonian system. God wants you to understand that you can be a King in the midst of that Babylonian system. He wants you to ascend to a place of kingship in the middle of your enemies. Ultimately, prayerfully, you will be able to represent the God who promoted you to that position.

Daniel, the Interpreter of Dreams

In Daniel, Chapter 2, we see things beginning to get remarkably interesting after these Hebrew boys are declared to be ten times better. We see a great story that's just the perfect set up for what God wants to do through Daniel for the rest of his life.

Daniel 2:1, "And in the second year of the reign of Nebuchadnezzar, Nebuchadnezzar dreamed dreams wherewith his spirit was troubled, and his sleep brake from him."

If you're serving under an unrighteous king, that king may have dreams that he will be unable to unlock. He or she may have dreams that will need to be interpreted. That role is reserved for a Daniel type believer. As we continue to go through this record, we'll see the reality of the Kingdom of God as opposed to the kingdom of men. The kingdom of men is always deficient in some way or another, and always in need of someone to solve problems. The Kingdom of God, on the other hand, has no inherent problems but is a problem solver. That is why the kingdom people are problem solvers! This King had a problem. He had dreams that were troubling him, but he could not interpret the dreams. He needed someone who could interpret his dreams. Now, mind you, he had an entire staff of soothsayers and magicians that claimed to be able to do things like interpret dreams. In reality, these men were as incapable of interpreting these particular dreams as the King was. Why? Because these dreams had their origin in the courts of Heaven. Therefore, only a representative of the God of Heaven would be able to interpret them.

Daniel 2:2, "Then the King commanded to call the magicians and the astrologers, and the sorcerers, and the Chaldeans, for to shew the King his dreams." Nebuchadnezzar was still tethered to his "B" team of magicians, astrologers, and sorcerers even though they continued to be unable to give him what he needed.

Daniel 2:3, "And the King said unto them, I have dreamed a dream, and my spirit was troubled to know the dream."

Daniel 2:4, "Then spake the Chaldeans to the King in Syriac, O King, live forever: tell thy servants the dream, and we will shew the interpretation." They wanted all the details so that they could know what kind of interpretation to put together.

Daniel 2:5, "The King answered and said to the Chaldeans, the thing is gone from me: if ye will not make known unto to me the dream, with the interpretation thereof, ye shall be cut in pieces and your houses shall be made a dunghill." In other words, the King is saying, "I don't just want somebody to try to interpret my dream after I've explained it to them. The dream is gone. I can't even remember the dream. I'll know that you really have a connection with God if you cannot just interpret the dream, but rather tell me the contents of the dream." He was calling them out.

Daniel 2:6, "But if you shew the dream, and the interpretation thereof, ye shall receive of me gifts and rewards, and great honour: therefore, shew me the dream and the interpretation thereof."

Daniel 2:7, "They answered again and said, Let the King tell his servants the dream, and we will shew the interpretation of it." I bet by this time they are shaking in their boots.

Daniel 2:8, "The King answered and said, I know of certainty that ye would gain the time because ye see the thing is gone from me." In other words, you're just trying to buy some time so that you will have some time to think something up.

Daniel 2:9 continues, "There is but one decree for you: for ye have prepared lying and corrupt words to speak before me, till the time be changed: therefore tell me the dream, and I shall know that ye can shew me the interpretation thereof." Wow! That's a tall order. One that only the true God can fill through the life of a submitted vessel. God wants some sons and daughters that can interpret dreams. The kings of the earth want the same.

Daniel 2:10, "And the Chaldeans answered before the king, and said, There is not a man upon the earth that can shew the king's matter; therefore, there is no king, lord, nor ruler, that asked such things at any magician, or astrologer, or Chaldean."

Daniel 2:11, "And it is a rare thing that the King requireth, and there is none other than can shew it before the king, except the gods, whose dwelling is not with flesh."

This reminds me of 1 Corinthians 2:14, "But the natural man receiveth not the things of the spirit of God: for they are foolishness unto him: neither can he know them, because they are spiritually discerned." These technicians of the spiritual realm had just run into a realm that was higher and greater than their capabilities. Their craft depended upon their ability to advise the King about spiritual matters that were beyond his control. But now, they are confronted with an assignment that went beyond their abilities. So, they told the King, that what he was asking was beyond the capacities of normal men. Furthermore, they said, only the gods can reveal something like this.

Well, they just told on themselves. They just said that as astrologers and magicians, even their gods weren't working in them on that level. But the Bible says that the true God reveals His secrets to His prophets. Daniel was a prophet of the Most High God, and God was about to show these counterfeit prophets the real capability of real prophets.

Let me just say this. The Devil isn't impressed with the fact that you dress up on Sunday and come to church. He isn't intimidated by that either. It's the power of God, the intelligence of God, the wisdom of God that intimidates the Devil, and his representatives. That's why we need to produce Daniel-type believers today. Some crises need a supernatural solution that can only come from the God of all creation. We are His representatives on the earth, and when people need that supernatural grace, they need to know where to find it. That's where we come into the picture. The Holy Spirit that dwells in us is the internal configuration from the God of creation, which enables us to have access to secrets from Heaven.

Daniel 2:12-17

"For this cause the King was angry and very furious and commanded to destroy all the wise men of Babylon. And the decree went forth that the wise *men* should be slain; and they sought Daniel and his fellows to be slain. Then Daniel answered with counsel and wisdom to Arioch, the captain of the king's guard, which was gone forth to slay the wise men of Babylon. He answered and said to Arioch the king's captain, 'Why is the decree so hasty from the king?' Then Arioch made the thing known to Daniel. Then Daniel went in and desired the King that he would give him time and that he would shew the King the interpretation. Then Daniel went to his house, and made the thing known to Hananiah, Mishael, and Azariah, his companions."

This King was intolerant of incompetence, and in his frustration, he commanded that all the wise men be destroyed, including Daniel and "his fellows." Now watch how Daniel responds to this threat. Rather than panicking and getting out of sorts emotionally, Daniel responded with "counsel and wisdom" Again, we see two of the seven spirits of God come into play, counsel, and wisdom. God always wants these seven spirits to be residing upon us and in us at all times because we never know when there will be a need for them. Daniel responded with counsel and wisdom. Where did it come from? It came from the spirit of God, who was at work in his life.

So after receiving divine counsel, Daniel, in the spirit of wisdom, requested of the King that he be given time and promised him that he would supply the answers to his request. Now that is an example of the faith, boldness, and confidence in the spirit of the Lord who was upon his life.

Daniel is granted that request. Now we must not pass over the gravity of this situation. Not only were all the wise men and soothsayers and astrologers in danger of being put to death, so was Daniel and his friends. So, Daniel, again walking in the wisdom of God, comes together with his three friends, and they intercede in prayer to God looking for the answers that the King seeks. Sometimes we just need to know when to find our intercessors and partner with them in our requests before the Lord.

Daniel wasn't trying to be the big man on campus. He had no pride in his ability to get an answer to his prayers by himself. Daniel knew that he needed someone to stand with him in prayer. I'm sure that Daniel said to them, "If we don't interpret the king's dreams, we're all going to be in trouble."

By all accounts, Daniel was the main guy among these four powerful princes. But he didn't allow his first-place position to interfere with his need to enlist help. This is a great lesson for those of us who serve in leadership positions. Headship doesn't mean that we do all things and everything alone. It just means that the buck stops with us. A leader needs to have the respect of his/her followers, and the quickest way to get respect is to respect those who you lead. Daniel respected the grace of prayer that also dwelled in the lives of his brothers. He included them in the process of acquiring the answer from God that they needed. They joined together as one to petition the Lord for insight, and God gave Daniel the Prophet among them, the answer that they all needed. May we all learn how to flow together as one when we need to access the mind of God.

Daniel 2:18-19, "That they would desire mercies of the God of Heaven concerning this secret; that Daniel and his fellows should not perish with the rest of the wise men of Babylon. Then was the secret revealed unto Daniel in a night vision. Then Daniel blessed the God of Heaven."

This reminds me of a Verse in the book of Job, about one of the significant ways that God speaks to us, in Job 33:15-17, "In a dream, a vision of the night, when sound sleep falls on men, while they slumber in their beds. Then He opens the ears of men, and seals their instruction, that He may turn man aside from his conduct, and keep man from pride."

The Word of the Lord says God speaks to us in the night season. Many of you have experienced this personally. Perhaps God has come to you with revelation via a vision in the middle of the night. If you have experienced that, then perhaps you can understand what Daniel must have experienced. God answered the prayers of Daniel and his friends, and because of that, Daniel was able to interpret the King's dream. And all the magicians and astrologers, and soothsayers, were spared from death because of the prayers of these men in whom the spirit of the true God dwelt.

There are perplexing dreams and global issues of great weight that the Kings of the earth are wrestling with. They all need a Daniel in their lives. They all need real solutions to problems of great gravity. Are we raising up the prince, the princess, the king, queen, the priest who can help them?

CHAPTER SIX

DANIEL AND SEVEN SPIRITS OF GOD

SEVERAL YEARS AGO, MY WIFE AND I WATCHED A MOVIE called *Limitless*. It was a pretty provocative movie where the main character could take a pill and tap into the 75 or 85 percent of his brain that most people don't use. I'm not sure how safe that would be or how scientifically or medically accurate the movie was, but it sure was fascinating to watch. But I take it one step further. I believe there are untapped parts of our brain we can access without resorting to drugs. I think there are latent aspects of the mind and spirit that are never used, because they only come awake and alive when we access them through the spirit of God. Access to this Divine technology will help us to become ten times better in our representation of the King of Kings.

This is where the seven spirits of God become all-important. Let's take a look at these seven spirits listed in Isaiah 11 before we look at them in operation in the life of Daniel.

"And the spirit of the LORD shall rest upon him,

The spirit of wisdom and understanding,

The spirit of counsel and might,

The spirit of knowledge and of the fear of the LORD. " Isaiah 11:2 (KJV).

The seven spirits, as listed above, are:

1. The spirit of the Lord
2. The spirit of wisdom
3. The spirit of understanding
4. The spirit of counsel
5. The spirit of might
6. The spirit of knowledge
7. The spirit of the fear of the Lord

These seven spirits are available to every believer through the Holy Spirit. I go into great detail about these seven spirits in my book, *The Seven Spirits of God: Learning to Walk in the Dominion and Authority of Christ*. This section of scripture in Isaiah 11 is speaking prophetically about the Lord Jesus Christ. This Verse states explicitly that these seven spirits would rest (remain) upon Him. These seven spirits were literally God's heavenly technology at work in the life of Jesus so that He could accurately and effectively represent His Heavenly Father while on the earth.

Nebuchadnezzar knew that he wanted the sharpest of the sharp from among his Hebrew captors. Yet, he had no idea that he was going to encounter a group of supernatural geniuses. The prophet Daniel is one of only a few men in whom we can document the presence of each of the seven spirits in his life.

Before we explore the presence of these seven spirits in the life and ministry of Daniel, lets briefly define each of them:

1. The spirit of the Lord - The Spirit of the Lord is the "I am" of God. It is the aspect of the character of God who displays and imparts the identity, authority, and dominion of the spirit of the God who is unshakable in its magnificence and authority.

2. The spirit of wisdom - The spirit of wisdom is the aspect of the character of God who imparts His skill, strategy, ability to apply knowledge accurately, creativity, and practical ingenuity.

3. The spirit of understanding - The spirit of understanding is the aspect of the character of God who imparts discernment and enables things that are separate and distinct to converge and flow together.

4. The spirit of counsel - The spirit of counsel is the aspect of the character of God who imparts the ability to impart the advice of God, the plans of God, and the counsel of God.

5. The spirit of might - The spirit of might is the aspect of the character of God that imparts the power and the strength of God into people and circumstances.

6. The spirit of knowledge - The spirit of knowledge is the aspect of the character of God who imparts the intelligence of God communicating information that is superior to the intellectual capacity of the natural man.

7. The spirit of the fear of the Lord - The Spirit of the fear of the Lord imparts the reverential fear of God that causes men to worship Him and to honor Him.

In the first two chapters of this story of Daniel and Hananiah, Mishael, and Azariah, we have seen the spirit of knowledge in the following verses: 1:4, 17; 2:21, 22, 25, 26, 28, 29, 30. We see the spirit of wisdom in the following verses:1:4, 17, 20; 2:14, 20, 21, 23, and 30. We find the spirit of understanding in the following verses: 1:4, 17, 20; 2:21, 30. We find the spirit of counsel in the following verses: 2:14. We see the spirit of might in the following verses: 2:20, 23, 37. We see the spirit of the fear of the Lord in the following verses: 1:8; 2:19, 20.

Taking a look at these records, we can begin to see a display of how significant the seven spirits of God were in the life and ministry of Daniel.

In Daniel 2:20, we pick up on the record when Daniel is giving praise to God for having answered his prayers. Verse 20, "Daniel answered and said, Blessed, be the name of God forever for wisdom and might are his..."

We are seeing two of the seven spirits of God again - wisdom and might. Wisdom begins with God, and here Daniel highlights two specific spirits of God that are wisdom and might. It's interesting that these two spirits are mentioned concerning the interpreting of the King's dream. I believe that these two spirits are still crucial to operating in the realm of the interpretation of dreams.

Apparently, Daniel and his friends were praying in an awfully specific and strategic way. Daniel needed the wisdom of God to unlock and interpret the King's dream, and he needed the might, the power and authority of God to engage in the spiritual warfare needed to break free from the interpretation from the grip of the principalities and powers that did not want that information to be released.

Here we get an understanding of the application and execution of these seven spirits of God. They are literally technologies of the spirit of God for accessing heaven's resources. Daniel was already a wise man, but he needed wisdom on another level to interpret this riddle. They accessed the spirit of might through aggressive prayer. Prayer is one of the most neglected weapons of spiritual warfare. We don't exercise spiritual muscle through natural weapons. In 2 Corinthians 10:4, it says that the weapons of our warfare are not carnal, but mighty through God to the pulling down of strongholds. They engaged in spiritual warfare, bombarding Heaven in prayer. They probably prayed all night, but as a result of engaging with the spirit of might, God revealed the secret to them.

Daniel 2:21, "And he changeth the times and the seasons." Daniel needed God to change his time and season. It wasn't time for him to die, and it wasn't the season for him to fail. I'm sure many of us could tell story after story of how God has intervened in our lives to change a time or a season. We praise God for His love, mercy, and preeminent power. The Devil wanted to destroy us, but God changed our time and season!

Daniel 2:21 continued, "He removeth kings and setteth up kings." Sometimes we need to be reminded of the sovereignty of God. Try as we may, there are some things that we are powerless to change. This verse says that God removes Kings and sets up Kings. That's a tough pill to swallow if your favorite person doesn't win an election, but scripture is replete with references about this subject, God sets up and removes kings, like it or not.

Daniel 2:21 says, "He giveth wisdom unto the wise." God doesn't give wisdom to fools. How unwise and uncomely it would be to give wisdom to a fool. God doesn't cast His pearls before swine. He is too wise for that. So, He gives (supernatural) wisdom to those who have already demonstrated a love for wisdom. (Proverbs 8:17)

Daniel 2:2, "And knowledge to them that know understanding." This isn't natural knowledge that anyone can get from reading a book. God gives supernatural knowledge of secret things to those who "know understanding." Why would God give us knowledge of something that we don't have the capacity to understand? These three, the spirits of knowledge, wisdom, and understanding, are so inextricably linked together in scripture that it is difficult to separate them. One leans on and is supported by the other. And you will find them working together in many instances in scripture.

> Daniel 2:22, "He revealeth the deep and secret things: He knoweth what is in the darkness, and the light dwelleth with Him."

> Daniel 2:23, "I thank thee, and praise thee, O' thou God of my fathers, who hast given me wisdom and might, and hast made known unto me now what we desired for thee: for thou hast now made known unto us the king's matter."

What an incredible record we have here of a prophet of the Lord providing insight into the spiritual technology of dream interpretation. This same access is available to the people of God today. If you are a dreamer and you have had difficulty interpreting the dreams that you receive, this would be a good segment of scripture to meditate on, study, and pray through.

> Daniel 2:24, "Therefore, Daniel went in unto Arioch, whom the King had ordained to destroy the wise *men* of Babylon: he went and said thus unto him; Destroy not the wise *men* of Babylon: bring me in before the king, and I will shew unto the King the interpretation."

Daniel 2:25, "Then Arioch brought in Daniel before the King in haste, and said thus unto him, I have found a man of the captives of Judah, that will make known unto the King the interpretation." The King said to Daniel.

Daniel 2:26, "The King answered and said to Daniel... Art thou able to make known unto me the dream which I have seen, and the interpretation thereof?"

Daniel 2:27, "Daniel answered in the presence of the king, and said, the secret which the King hath demanded cannot the wise men, the astrologers, the magicians, the soothsayers, shew unto the king."

Daniel 2:28, "But there is a God in Heaven that revealeth secrets."

What a dramatic moment. This moment would save the lives of all the King's wise men and change the direction of a nation. These are the kind of moments that still need to happen in our world today. Daniel served the same God who we serve, and His desire to work through His people has not been abated.

I remember a prophetess who came to our spiritual house many years ago. She prophesied to a couple and talked about their bedroom and the inside of their house. She described it with accurate detail. She said that she saw something in this corner of the room, and it was exactly where she said it was. By the time she finished speaking with such accuracy, they were all ears. That word changed their lives that night. This is the kind of sharp, prophetic revelation and insight that Daniel had. Daniel said, "Do you know what? I see your thoughts that came into your head while you were in bed." Wow, now that's a prophet of God.

In a display of great humility, Daniel said in verse 30, "This secret is not revealed to me because I have more wisdom than any living, but for their sakes that shall make known the interpretation to the king, and that thou mightiest know the thoughts of thy heart." Wow! What a spirit of humility. Not beating his chest with bragging, but simply deflecting attention from himself to call attention to the purposes of God.

Daniel received a revelation to interpret this dream. It was a particularly important dream that impacted more than Nebuchadnezzar and his kingdom. This dream was pertaining to a time far exceeding his life and applicable to the end times.

You're going to run into people who you may work with whom God desires to bring into the Kingdom. But God is really waiting for somebody to come along, who's walking by the Spirit of the Lord, to speak a Word to that individual. Not just, "Oh, come to my church next week." No! I'm talking about a prophetic word, a piercing word that will shift their lives from darkness to light.

Daniel 2:46, "Then the King Nebuchadnezzar fell upon his face."

Oh, my goodness. When was the last time someone fell on their face when you prophesied to them? This word must have hit him right in the heart. Interestingly, there is a Verse in the *New Testament* that parallels this experience. Perhaps we have fallen short of genuine prophetic release in or modern times. Here's the scripture, from 1 Corinthians 14:24–25, "But if all prophesy, and there come in one that believeth not, or one unlearned, he is convinced of all, he is judged of all: And thus are the secrets of his heart made manifest; and so falling down on his face he will worship God and report that God is in you of a truth." (KJV) Now back to Daniel.

> Daniel 2:46, "Then the King Nebuchadnezzar fell upon his face and worshipped Daniel and commanded that they should offer an oblation and sweet odours unto him."

> Daniel 2:47, "The King answered unto Daniel, and said Of a truth *it is*, that you God is a God of gods, and a Lord of kings, and a revealer of secrets, seeing thou couldest reveal this secret."

> Daniel 2: 48, "Then the King made Daniel a great man, and gave him many great gifts, and made him ruler over the whole province of Babylon, and chief of the governors over all the wise men of Babylon."

> Daniel 2:49, "Then Daniel requested of the king, and he set Shadrach, Meshach, and Abednego, over

the affairs of the province of Babylon: but Daniel *sat* in the gate of the king."

This was the goal of God's dealings with Daniel. It was already in the mind of God that Daniel would be a King in Babylon. But Daniel had to go through the process. He had to go on the journey with God, walking much of that journey in sheer faith because Daniel did not know what the final destination would be. Isn't that so familiar with how God deals with us? Many of us have taken so many journeys with God, not fully knowing the final destination but merely trusting the Lord that He will cause us to triumph in Christ.

After we endure the process, God wants us to step into our rightful place as kings and queens, and princes, and princesses in the earth. That looks different for all of us. Kingship for me is different from kingship for you. God wants us to be set apart to be used by Him in every sphere of culture and society. This was the frame of mind that Daniel had. His response to promotion was not selfish. Instead of accepting the promotion alone, Daniel reminds the King that he has three friends who are also anointed, also full of wisdom, and have also successfully completed his training program with the additional certification from the God of Heaven and earth. The King's response was to set Shadrach, Meshach, and Abednego, over the affairs of the province of Babylon. This is the end result of the presence of the seven spirits of God in the lives of these young leaders, and this is the prototype of the modern-day order of kings and priests that we are to be according to 1 Peter 2:9 and Revelation 1:6.

A Note: One of the objectives of this book is to light a fire for equipping our youth with a new set of spiritual values. The Creator of the universe has established principles and protocols that are designed to develop His people into leaders and workers who advance His Kingdom on earth. When we develop young people who know who they are in Christ and learn how to walk with authority and dominion in any sphere of life, we can fulfill the prayer of Jesus, "Thy kingdom come, thy will be done in the earth as it is in Heaven." (Matthew 6:10)

God needs more Daniels and friends who will walk with Him through life without compromise. Challenge yourself to be a kingmaker. Youth all over the world are waiting for you.

CHAPTER SEVEN

FIVE PRINCIPLES OF THE TEN TIMES BETTER LIFE

THROUGHOUT THIS BOOK, WE HAVE DISCUSSED THE lifestyle of Daniel, Shadrach, Meshach, and Abednego. I have described this as the ten times better lifestyle. In this chapter, I'll highlight five key principles of the ten times better life that I have extracted from their lives.

Principle #1: The World is Looking for Gifted People

One of the first things that we see in the very first chapter of Daniel is the premium that leaders place upon high capacity potential. King Nebuchadnezzar took the children of Israel captive and immediately proceeded to select the youth with the greatest potential for service in his courts. In verses 3 and 4 of Daniel

Chapter 1, the scriptures present a list of the qualities that he was looking for in these youths. The list clearly indicates that he was looking for the best of the best. This must also be the standard for the body of Christ. But we shouldn't just be looking for the best; we should be producing the best. The spiritual enabling that we receive through the indwelling power of the Holy Spirit gives us a competitive advantage over all others. Literally, the spirit of the living God lives inside of us.

Greatness in people doesn't just happen; it is developed. Champions *are made,* not merely born. For every person who becomes the best in their field, hundreds missed the mark. Often, those who missed the mark have greater potential and sometimes innate ability, but for some reason, they were never developed. Developing the latent potential in our emerging leaders should be imperative in every Christ-community on the planet. If it's true that every organization rises or falls on the quality of its leadership, then developing high capacity leaders is a must for the 21st-century church.

The qualities that Nebuchadnezzar listed were qualities that the King valued, and therefore, he wanted those qualities in the lives of those who were to serve him in his government. Being gifted was not enough. Nebuchadnezzar wanted those who were gifted but who were also quick learners, could speak his language, who looked royal, who could represent him well, and who would serve his God. We, the Body of Christ, should be looking for the same qualities in those that we develop to serve our God. Finally, the spirit of the Lord, coupled with one's natural and spiritual abilities, will be a catalyst for greatness.

Principle #2: The Fear of the Lord

Believe it or not, it is possible to serve in Babylon without becoming like Babylon. Daniel and his friends understood this principle. Despite the immediate threat of possible loss of life, they all stood together to say resolutely, "We will not eat the king's meat." Sometimes refusing to compromise will cause you immediate pain. At other times difficulties may arise that have to be overcome. But, standing on the truth and for the truth has reward not just in this life, but also for all of eternity. Daniel requested that they he permitted forgoing the King's meat, not simply because he preferred pulse. He was concerned that eating the King's meat would cause them to defile themselves. They were willing to possibly sacrifice their relationship with the King to stand for what they believed in.

The significant spiritual principle in play in this situation is the practical presence of the fear of the Lord. The fear of the Lord causes the heart of man to reverence God in such a way that he is "afraid" to disobey Him, disappoint Him, disturb Him, or in any way, "cross" him. It's the same sense of awe that causes us to worship Him. Daniel, Mishael, Meshach, and Azariah refused to compromise on their convictions because of their fear of the Lord. As I articulated previously, the fear of the Lord is the seventh of the seven spirits of God listed in Isaiah

11:2. There are things that the flesh of man would love to do, but the spirit of man realizes that it cannot move forward on the desires of the flesh because the fear of the Lord is so dominant in that person, that they can only do what the Lord would have them do. This is what we were seeing in the lives of Daniel and his friends. The fear of the Lord is the "why" behind, "But Daniel purposed in his heart that he would not defile himself with the portion of the king's meat, or with the wine which he drank." This is also what we must see in the lives of the people of God in this season.

Principle #3: The Practical Presence of the Seven Spirits of God

Back in Chapter 6, I presented an overview of the seven spirits of God in the life and ministries of Daniel. In this book, we see all seven of the seven spirits in operation. As we endeavor to develop ten times better contingent of the believer, the seven spirits of God will need to be familiar territory to every believer. These seven spirits are hidden in the scriptures if one is not aware that they exist. Yet God has laced them throughout the text of His word and caused them to be readily available to the seeking heart. One of the most practical books in the Bible has the most frequent mentions of all seven of these seven spirits. That is the book of Proverbs.

By way of demonstration, I will show you the presence of these seven spirits in the book of Proverbs, in verses in Chapter 1 alone:

1. Verse 2 - the spirits of knowledge, wisdom, and understanding
2. Verse 3 - the spirit of wisdom
3. Verse 4 - the spirit of knowledge
4. Verse 5 - the spirits of wisdom, understanding, and counsel
5. Verse 6 - the spirits of understanding and wisdom
6. Verse 7 - the spirits of the fear of the Lord, knowledge, and wisdom
7. Verse 20 - the spirit of wisdom
8. Verse 22 - the spirit of knowledge
9. Verse 23 - the spirit of the Lord and the spirit of knowledge
10. Verse 25 - the spirit of counsel
11. Verse 29 - the spirit of knowledge and the spirit of the fear of the Lord
12. Verse 30 - the spirit of counsel

The only one of the seven spirits not listed in Chapter 1 of Proverbs is the spirit of might. That, I believe, is due to the message being conveyed in this Chapter, which is the need for mankind to first to learn to lean on God and forgo any sense of power or authority that they possess apart from Him!

A review of subsequent chapters will demonstrate the prevalence of these seven spirits in the book of Proverbs. These seven spirits are fundamental to walking in the power and authority of Heaven, and they are as available to us as simply reading through one book of Proverbs and applying the principles thereof. Daniel and his three friends walked in this dimension, and so must we.

Principle #4: Be Spiritually Ambidextrous

In the ten times better lifestyle, the people of God are spiritually ambidextrous. Ambidextrous means that rather than favoring one hand or the other, as is common, you are equally proficient with both your left and right hands.

Now, these sons of God, Daniel, Shadrach, Meshach, and Abednego demonstrated that they were spiritually ambidextrous. They knew the learning and the language of the Chaldeans, but they also stayed true to living the life of God. We need people who are spiritually ambidextrous in this age of emerging kings and priests. We want to develop men and women who are not foreign to matters of culture or their environment while keeping in tune with the spirit realm. As a matter of fact, they are even more attuned to what's happening in both realms so that they will be more effective in promulgating the purposes of the Kingdom of God. The King of Babylon meant to train Daniel and his friends so that they would be useful in his kingdom. But God had different plans. Similar to Moses and Joseph, God permitted Daniel to enter into a hostile environment under less than desirable circumstances.

A study of the scriptures will show that this scenario is not an uncommon strategy in the ways of God. The people of God were never meant to be exclusively equipped for religious service. God's plan was always to have a kingdom of priests who would serve him in the services of the sanctuary and the marketplace. This is the king-priest and royal priesthood principles of Revelations 1:6, and 1 Peter 2:9. So, to prepare these mighty men of God for service in Babylon, God caused Babylon to train them, not knowing that they had been sent by God to ascend their ranks and occupy places of authority. God is still sending undercover agents into Babylon today. Are you one of God's undercover agents of the kingdom?

Principle #5: Your Faith Will be Tested

Every great Patriarch of the Bible had a walk of faith with God and that faith was always tested. Fear will test your faith. Fatigue will test your faith. Opposition will test your faith. Betrayal will test your faith. The love of money will test your faith. Relationships will test your faith. Health challenges will test your faith. Financial trials will test your faith. The lust of the eyes will test your faith. The jealousy of others will test your faith. Many things will test your faith before you ever get to the promise.

These sons of God were functioning like kings and priests despite captivity. No prison can hold you back. No bars can prevent you. As a matter of fact, Paul did some of his best writing in prison. It's not about the prison you're in; it's about the way you act inside the prison. How do you behave in the prison? What happens when you get closed in on every side? What happens when you are put in lock up? What happened to Daniel when they were in prison? Daniel and those Hebrew boys became *10 Times Better*—while being in prison!

What happened to Peter? Peter was in prison, and he started singing the song of the Lord, and an angel showed up. (I won't even begin to count all the suffering Paul endured, yet stayed the course in his work for the Lord—and there's an entire book of the Bible devoted to what Job went through and never lost faith in almighty Jehovah.) Are you still singing the song of the Lord even though you have a situation in your life that you believe is captivity? Are you still singing, or are you complaining? You'd better start singing the song of the Lord because God is watching you and taking note of the way you act amid that captivity. The prison can take many forms. It can be emotional, it can be physical, or it can be financial.

Sometimes, you can't avoid captivity. Jesus couldn't avoid being taken captive because it was part of God's plan. But sometimes, you're taken captive, and God doesn't deliver you. Why doesn't He deliver you? Because there's a lesson in the turmoil that you need to learn. God could have delivered Peter before he even got locked up. He chose not to, however, so Peter got locked up. While he was locked up, he had to sing the song of the Lord. What was God trying to get out of him? The song of the Lord. He wouldn't have been singing the song of the Lord if he had avoided captivity. Now, sometimes God will deliver you out of captivity, but when He doesn't, sing the song of the Lord. When your finances get locked up, tithe anyway because God's watching you. He's trying to see how you behave during captivity. If you stop giving during captivity, don't expect Him to give you favor with that next promotion. God is trying to teach us how-to walk-through adversity without compromising our spiritual values. Never stop applying the principles of God just because you step into a place of captivity.

Daniel and his friends were tested in their faith, and they stood firm on the promises of God and passed through the tests. There is a lifestyle that grows accustomed to faith being tested. This is the lifestyle of faith. Numerous scriptures and examples are given to us in the scriptures about the journey of faith. The entirety of Chapter 11 of Hebrews is dedicated to Biblical heroes of faith. All were tested, some received the promise in their lifetimes, others did not. For those who did not receive their expected end in their lifetimes, there are eternal rewards reserved for them.

Tests are like temptations. James 1:2 says, "My brethren, count it all joy when ye fall into diverse temptations." What kind of joy is that? It's the same kind of joy Jesus had when He was on the cross, and He endured that shame for us. His greatest reward came after death. Many of us will have a greater reward after death than the rewards of this life. That's a hard pill to swallow unless you have a state of mind that embraces eternity. A mindset that embraces eternity believes that this life is but a temporary journey to an eternal destination. When you step into a lion's den, or a fiery furnace, with the expectation that God will deliver you, you must have an eternal mindset. Jesus did not fear death because he literally believed that God would raise him from the dead. And the Father has given us the same promise. One of the most destructive things ever to strong faith is the fear of death. That could mean the death of a relationship, death of your finances, or even death of your physical life. Fear is the great enemy of faith. And so, God repeatedly tells us not to fear the death of anything because He has ensured that we are more than conquerors in all these things (Romans 8:37-39).

Why don't you put God to the test? Prove Him to yourself. Don't say you'll try to do the will of God; say you're going to do the will of God. Try is coded language setting you up for a copout. Saying, "I'm going to do it" is an assurance. The people who say they are going to do it, get there quicker than the folks who merely "try" to do it.

Too often, we talk ourselves out of our faith. But understand that the walk of faith has a lot of rough patches sometimes. In every instance of Daniel's walk of faith, he had to pass some kind of test. If we are to be successful in raising people who are ten times better, we must train them to be prepared for trials, tests, and difficulties. The ten times better life will be a life of tests, trials, and difficulties—all overcome by faith!

CHAPTER EIGHT

TEN TIMES BETTER IN THE LION'S DEN

I N DANIEL, CHAPTER 6, WE FIND AN AMAZING RECORD OF one of the highlights of Daniel's ten times better way of life. Daniel served three kings during his lifetime, and his walk with God was transformative in the administration of each king. This Chapter has some amazing God-moments for our learning.

Daniel 6:1, "It pleased Darius to set over the kingdom a hundred and twenty princes, which should be over the whole kingdom."

Verse 6:2, "And over these three presidents; of whom Daniel was first: that the princes might give accounts unto them, and the King should have no damage."

King Darius was an extraordinarily strong leader who established a leadership team of one hundred and twenty princes. One hundred and twenty is a significant number. One reason for its significance Biblically is that it is a multiple of twelve (12), the number for government, and ten (10), the number of orders. So this team provided a strong governmental order for the King. Three Presidents governed these princes, and Daniel was the first among equals. This structure provided for the King a system of accountability and minimized the possibility of loss. How significant was it that Daniel, after serving three gentile Kings, was still functioning at a high governmental level and still had the confidence of these Kings to serve at such a high level?

This strategy also highlights two "apostolic" principles of governing: accountability to the "set" leaders and protection of the set leaders' anointing by setting in place a strong leadership team who understands that the destiny of the organism lies in the preservation of the leader.

> Daniel 6:3, "Then this Daniel was preferred above the presidents and princes, because an excellent spirit was in him; and the King thought to set him over the whole realm."

Here we have another powerful revelation of the *ten times better life*. Daniel was preferred, not because he was handsome, not because he was wealthy, not because he was politically well connected, not because he paid favors, and not because he was a good team player. Daniel was preferred (most desired among a group) even above the presidents and princes, because "an excellent [exceptional; preeminent] spirit was in him." Now that's the way to represent God and the King! Coupled with his other exceptional qualifications, Daniel possessed a spirit of excellence that caused him to stand out from even the other two Presidents.

> Daniel 6:4, "Then the presidents and princes sought
> to find occasion against Daniel."

One of the unfortunate consequences of being ten times better is the jealousy, envy, and resentment that may arise in the heart of those who serve with you or for you. We find this present in the hearts of the other presidents and princes. This kind of warfare is common for those who operate at this high level of excellence. Nehemiah encountered this in Sanballat and Tobiah when he was building the walls of Jerusalem. This animosity in their hearts caused them to seek to "find an occasion against Daniel." In other words, they were looking for a fault or a mistake, or some reason to bring an accusation against Daniel. If you're in leadership or you're connected to the King, or the set man in your church or business, beware. There are people who will try to tear you down or have you removed from your position. There is an adversary who constantly seeks to kill, still, and destroy.

Daniel 6:4 says, "They sought to find occasion against Daniel concerning the kingdom; but they could find no occasion nor fault; forasmuch as he was faithful, neither was there any error or fault found in him."

It was difficult to find fault against Daniel because he was faithful, and there was no error nor fault found in him. That's a pretty awesome resume. That's functioning at a high level of excellence, competence, and integrity. Daniel's defense against the spirit of excellence that he walked in.

Daniel 6:5, "Then said these men, we shall not find any occasion against this Daniel, except we find it against him concerning the law of his God."

Daniel 6:6, "Then these presidents and princes assembled together to the king, and said thus unto him, King Darius, live forever."

Daniel 6:7, "All the presidents of the kingdom, the governors, and the princes, the counselors, and the captains, have consulted together to establish a royal statute, and to make a firm decree, that whosoever shall ask a petition of any God or man for thirty days, save of thee, O king, he shall be cast into the den of lions."

Daniel 6:8, "Now, oh king, establish the decree, and sign the writing, that it be not changed, according to the law of the Medes and Persians, which altereth not. Daniel 6:9, "Wherefore King Darius signed the writing and the decree."

What a devilish scheme designed to take down a righteous man! These leaders manipulated King Darius, who was unaware of their diabolical plot against his chief President. I wonder where Daniel was when this was presented. I wonder why the King didn't ask about him. I'm sure there was a scheme to cover that eventuality as well. King Darius signed the decree, and now his jealous colleagues knew they would find Daniel violating such a decree. Wickedness dwells in the hearts of men, and the right opportunity will bring it out.

Daniel 6:10, "Now when Daniel knew that the writing was signed, he went into his house; and his windows being open in his chamber toward Jerusalem, he kneeled upon his knees three times a day, and prayed, and gave thanks before his God, as he did aforetime."

Wow! What a man, this Daniel! "When he knew that the writing was signed," he went into his house and prayed three times a day. Reading this helps me to understand why we don't see many Daniels in our day. We just don't have many with the DNA of commitment, dedication, fortitude, and fear of the Lord like Daniel. Daniel's manner of life reflected the character of God, and this causes him to be a man who we must emulate. Where is the God of Daniel? He is looking for Daniels!

Daniel 6:11, "Then these men assembled, and found Daniel praying and making supplication before his God." (But of course, he was!)

Daniel 6:12, "They came near, and spake before the King concerning the king's decree; Hast though not signed a decree, that every man who shall ask a petition of any God or man within thirty days, save of thee, O king, shall be cast into the den of lions? The King answered and said, the thing is true, according to the law of Medes and Persians, which altereth not."

Daniel 6:13, "Then answered they and said before the king, That Daniel, which is of the children of the captivity of Judah, regardeth not thee, O King, nor the decree that thou hast signed, but maketh his petition three times a day."

Daniel 6:14, "Then the king, when he heard these words, was sore displeased with himself, and set his heart on Daniel to deliver him: and he labored to the going down of the sun to deliver him."

What a man, this King Darius! When he heard that Daniel was still worshipping his God, he didn't get angry with Daniel;

he got angry at himself for having been duped into signing such a decree. This speaks volumes about the kind of man who King Darius was. In his desperation to save Daniel, he labored all night, trying to see how he could reverse the irreversible - the King's decree.

Daniel 6:15, "Then these men assembled unto the king, and said unto the king, Know, O king, that the law of the Medes and the Persians is, That no decree nor statute which the King establisheth may be changed." In other words, "I don't know what you are laboring about, but you know this is the law, you signed it!"

Daniel 6:16, "Then the King commanded, and they brought Daniel, and cast him into the den of lions. Now the King spake and said unto Daniel." (This guy blows my mind. The King is encouraging Daniel while he's throwing him in the lion's den.) He "said unto Daniel, thy God whom thou servest continually, he will deliver thee." In other words, "I'm going to have to throw you in the den, Daniel, but remember your God's going to take care of you." Wow! That is incredible. Dairus must have also believed in the power of the God who Daniel served.

Daniel 6:17, "And a stone was brought, and laid upon the mouth of the den; and the King sealed it with his own signet, and with the signet of his lords; that the purpose might not be changed concerning Daniel."

Daniel 6:18, "Then the King went to his palace, and passed the night fasting neither were instruments of music brought before him: and his sleep went from him." (What? A Gentile King fasting for a Prophet of the Lord God of the Israelites?)

Daniel 6:19, "Then the King arose very early in the morning and went in haste unto the den of lions."

Daniel 6:20, "And when he came to the den, he cried with a lamentable voice unto Daniel: and the King spake and said to Daniel. O Daniel, servant of the living God, is thy God, whom thou servest continually, able to deliver thee from the lions?"

Again, this story speaks volumes, not only about Daniel but also about King Darius. He fated all night and went without sleep, praying for Daniel. A Gentile prayer warrior. At dawn, he got up and ran to the tomb to check on Daniel. My how Daniel's life must have impacted this King. My how he must have believed in Daniel's God.

Daniel 6:2, "Then said Daniel unto the king, O king, live forever."

Daniel 6:22, "My God, hath sent his angel, and hath shut the lions' mouths, that they have not hurt me forasmuch as before him innocence was found in me; and also before thee, O king, have I done no hurt."

Here we see that God intervened supernaturally for Daniel by sending an angel to stop the mouths of the lions. God still has angels who He can, and will, and does, dispatch to help us in times of need. Perhaps we haven't seen much angelic intervention because we haven't been willing to go to the last mile with God. Perhaps also, because, as we see in the next verse, innocence is not found in us.

Daniel said that God sent His angel to help him because He found "innocence" in him. The Hebrew word innocence means to be blameless, to be found without sin. This is another message about the significance of the condition of our character. I want to tell you that there are some things you won't be able to do with your own strength. Sometimes, God will have to send an angel to intervene on your behalf. The angels showed up to help Daniel on several occasions. This Prophet Daniel is a case study on walking with God in the integrity of faith and seeing Him show Himself strong on behalf of one of His sons. May we study and learn about the ways and the patterns of Daniel's walk with God?

Daniel 6:23, "Then was the King exceeding glad for him and commanded that they should take Daniel up out of the den. So Daniel was taken up out of the den, and no manner of hurt was found upon him, because he believed in his God."

Daniel 6:24, "And the King commanded, and they brought those men which had accused Daniel, and they cast them into the den of lions..."

Daniel remained faithful to God, and God was faithful to Daniel. Every time Daniel got into trouble, God delivered him. Every time that man tried to come against Daniel, God delivered him. Galatians 6:7 says, "Be not deceived God is not mocked for whatsoever ye sow that ye shall also reap." You reap what you sow. These guys had Daniel thrown in the lion's den, and the tables were turned on them. Previously, the guys who laid hands on Daniel were burned up with the fire. Now, we see the guys who threw Daniel into the lion's den end up in the lion's den with their entire families. Before they even reached the bottom of the den, the lions had consumed them.

Daniel 6:25, "Then King Darius wrote unto all people, nations, and languages, that dwell in the earth; Peace be multiplied unto you."

Daniel 6:26, "I make a decree, That in every dominion of my kingdom men tremble and fear before the God of Daniel: for he is the living God and steadfast forever and his kingdom that which shall not be destroyed and his dominion shall be even unto the end."

Daniel 6:27, "He delivereth and rescueth, and he wor-
keth signs and wonders in Heaven and in earth who
hath delivered Daniel from the power of the lions."

Daniel 6:28, "So this Daniel prospered in the reign
of Darius, and in the reign of Cyrus the Persian."

Wow, what a testimony from a gentile king. A King of Babylon was so impacted by the God of his President that he ends
up changing the laws of the land to accommodate Daniel's God.
And the result is that Daniel prospered for the remainder of his
reign, and so did the nation. This is all about that ten times better life that I've been speaking of. It's a life of triumph, though
not without trial. It's a life of preeminence, but not without a
price. But it is the life that God has called us to live. It is the life
of *ten times better*.

We're trying to impact people with the principles of the
kingdom, as demonstrated in the life of Daniel. Until you know
these things, and until you can navigate intelligently with wisdom, through the principles of the life of a Daniel, you can't
produce a Daniel. What God wants you and I to do is to produce Daniels. There are a lot of good programs out there today,
and a lot of great places that are endeavoring to minister to a
problem. As we've all heard before, we're not here to just solve
problems; we're here to create solutions. Create creatively. Spirit
of Wisdom, there is a solution in God, for this nation. There's a
solution for this city in God.

Despite what we do or don't see, there's a greater place in God that God wants for the United States of America. For a nation that has so many believers in it, as many people gathering in church on Sunday mornings as this nation does, God wants to impact this nation. We've got to have a Daniel rise up amid every community, and several Daniels wouldn't hurt a thing. Daniel must be ubiquitous. We've got to have men and women of integrity, excellence, intelligence, wisdom, and strategy. We've got to have young people who are not afraid to take a stand and say, "I'm not going to eat of the King's bread. I'm not going to drink of his wine because I have another assignment, and I am going to stay on assignment."

Do you know the interpretation of Daniel's name? It means "God is my judge." When your name means "God is my judge," you have to live a whole different way. Integrity has to be your middle name. When your first name is "God is my judge," that means when nobody else is watching, you know God is watching. When there's nobody else to answer to, you have to answer to Him.

If we want to endeavor to create a community of "God is my judge," Daniels, we must develop young people and adults who are men and women of integrity. It doesn't matter what everybody else does; you have to walk with integrity before God because that is the lifestyle of those who are ten times better.

May the Lord grant us the grace to develop men, women, and children once again in the pattern of Daniel. The world is waiting for the manifestation of the Sons of God and many of these sons have the Daniel-type grace and anointing upon their lives. We must cultivate a new breed of the Sons of God in this hour. Sons who take the mandate seriously to (re)build the old waste places and raise the foundations of many generations again. Sons who will literally be called the repairers of the breach, the restorer of paths to dwell in. Amen and Amen!

ABOUT THE AUTHOR

APOSTLE ERIC L. WARREN IS THE FOUNDER OF EQUIPPERS CITY Church, Equip Charlotte, and Eric L. Warren Ministries. His ministries are committed to developing and release men and women of spiritual maturity so that they will represent Christ in the earth. The ministry headquarters are located in Columbus, Ohio. Apostle Warren holds degrees in Sociology, Philosophy, and Theology.

Called and commissioned as a Pastor, Teacher, and Apostle, Apostle Warren is appreciated for his sensitivity to the Holy Spirit, and his keen insight into the Word of God. Having served in ministry for more than four decades, he has been graced by God with a father's heart and the ability to train and develop leaders for effective and excellent service in the Body of Christ. His leadership development class, called Body Builders, has produced many competent leaders who currently serve the body of Christ and the marketplace with excellence and integrity. He is the author of three books, the most recent being *Character, The Path that God Walks*, which has received rave reviews.

Apostle Warren has been married to his wife Carolyn for over 49 years, and they have three adult daughters, four grandchildren, and one great-grandchild. They recently relocated to Charlotte, N.C. from Columbus, Ohio.